WALKING THROUGH THE VALLEY
My extended journey

JOEL DOUTRE

Publisher: JEBCA Editions
A division of JEBCA Ministries, Inc.
www.jebcaeditions.org
jebcaeditions@gmail.com / info@jebcaeditions@org

Author: Joel Doutre (joeldoutre@verizon.net)

Editing: Donna Ferrier

Book Cover Design: Shay Culligan

Photos: Carine Doutre & Frantz Jean Baptiste

Legal Deposit: 2018 (Library of Congress)
ISBN 10: 1-68084-059-2
ISBN 13: 978-1-68084-059-9

18 19 20 21 22 23 JEBCA 10 9 8 7 6 5 4 3 2 1

Library of Congress Control Number: 2017959665

Printed in the United States of America

Blessed is the man whose strength is in you, whose heart is set on pilgrimage. As they pass through the Valley of Baca, they make it a spring. The rain also covers it with pools.

Psalm 84: 5-6

4 | Walking through the Valley

In loving memory of my father

Charles Desmornes Doutre, my hero of the faith

TABLE OF CONTENTS

ABOUT THE AUTHOR

Joel Doutre, formerly Joel Desmornes, is a well-known radio host and master of ceremonies in our community. Born and raised in Haiti, Joel  was one of the youngest broadcasters in the late 70s at *Radio Lumière*, a network of radio stations started by *World Team Mission*. He managed to secure his position as a board operator/on-air talent while he was still a high school senior at Lycée Toussaint Louverture. Widely known for his radio show *Chante la Kay*, featuring popular Christian music, he was soon promoted to production director, whose functions included writing; producing; and editing audio drama and public service announcements.

After he left Haiti in the 80s, Joel lived in Florida just for a few months. His father, Reverend Charles Desmornes Doutre, who was a church minister in Montreal then, advised him to move to Boston. Upon moving to Boston, he gladly rejoined his former co-workers Jonel Dalexis and Samuel Laborde to extend their radio ministry on foreign land. They teamed up to bring to thousands of Massachusetts listeners a glimmer of Radio Lumière's programming on WEZE 1260 AM. Joel has made a name for himself being one of the trailblazers of our broadcasting organization Echo Evangélique, grown over the years to a radio station on 88.9 FM SCA.

The man with a golden voice who had served the Christian community in Haiti is still worth of listening to abroad because of his passion, enthusiasm, and professionalism in broadcasting. I especially value Joel for his integrity and his dependability. When he says yes, he means yes, regardless of the odds against him. If I were to use the Lord's word to David when He called him the man after His own heart, I would say: "I have found in Joel the man after my own heart" given his unwavering commitment and dedication to Echo Evangélique since 1983.

Joel's services provided in the community at large are not limited to broadcasting. He has served at other levels. His numerous years spent in public education working with students and parents earned him a lot of respect within the teaching profession. Joel is also a loving father and husband who has devoted his life to the physical, financial, and spiritual well-being of his family. He is man of conviction, courage and strength with the knack for serving in multiple domains.

Unfortunately, at the end of 2014 and mostly in 2015, Joel was no longer quite active. He became ill with a chronic disease that crippled his normal functions. I witnessed his pain and suffering when he was in the hospital. There was a time, it seemed all hope was lost. Nevertheless, his unrelenting faith in God, his spiritual strength, and his positive spirit helped him to overcome his misfortune. By 2016, his doctors confirmed that has been completely healed. Joel was absolutely right when he said to his wife Carine during a prayer meeting before he was admitted in September 2014: "You know your husband is a trooper."

What a mighty and faithful God we serve! Despite our unfaithfulness, He never ceases to amaze us by doing remarkable things in our lives while sitting on His throne. We can never go wrong with God. "He guides me along the right paths for his name's sake" (Psalm 23:3). To God be the glory!

Jonel Dalexis
Echo Evangélique, General Manager

ACKNOWLEDGEMENTS & SPECIAL THANKS

Making the decision to write this book was easily influenced by two community leaders: Jean Samuel Trézil and Reverend Jean Joel Manassé Louis. When I first told Louis my personal story at the Braintree Mall Joe's Restaurant in early 2016 during a special luncheon, he pointed out: "my friend, you should write a book." A month later, I ran into Trézil at Boston Neighborhood Network Television (BNNTV) studio, where I was invited to have a live interview with Tele Kreyol host Charlot Lucien. After watching with amazement my testimony in the engineering studio, Trézil approached me and said: "Joel, you have more than enough material to write a book."

Once I introduced the idea to Carine Doutre, my wife of 22 years, she was ecstatic. "Honey, I am behind you 100%, and I promised you full support," she exclaimed. Carine, whom I consider a gift from Heaven, was really instrumental in

helping me chronicle certain events that had occurred in the intensive care unit. Since I could only recount things I had witnessed, my wife became a source of inspiration, considering everything she had watched me go through during the whole terrifying ordeal. Without having her sitting by my side on many occasions, I would have never been able to put on paper my whole story.

I also owe a debt of gratitude to Frantz Jean Baptiste for providing in his book, Mémoire Parlante des Leaders Evangéliques Haïtiens (Volume 1), a summary of my personal life and experiences, which has served as a prelude to my publication. I am indebted to Frantz for being the first penman, enabling readers to catch a glimpse of my story in French.

Carine and I want to extend our appreciation and sincerest thanks to family members on both sides: Antoinette, Natacha, Yvrose, Joey, Pélo, Naomie, Juny, Ketty, Patrick, Nick, Serges, Jacqueline, Gladys, Luc, Chantal, Lude, Marie André, Marie Carme, Sista Evangéliste and others. How can we forget those who showed us their love over a long period of time? If my memory serves me well, I do remember friends and colleagues like Reverend Rosemond Antoine and spouse, Reverend Jéroboam Tismé and spouse, Reverend Ewald Delva, Reverend Jean Pierre Carné, Paulaine Délice and her late husband Jean Hermès, Gertrude Thélusma, Jacqueline Sénat, Manitha Mantoban, Willia Henry, Schesky Juste, Matthieu Guerrier, Guitone Atimy, Joseph Lucien Auguste, Thérèse Emile, Lorvil and Mona Dorvil, Mona Vallon, Charlie Péant, Doctor Soliny Védrine, Reverend Serges Joseph, Reverend Exénor Février, Reverend Varnel Antoine, Edna Laurore, Jonel Dalexis, Hubert Dalexis, Beaudy Homicile, Wilner Auguste, Eunice Brutus, Fritzner Filoma, Jean Joseph and Solange Normil, Marie Mirca Tangard Cayemite, Carlot and Raymonde Saintristil, Eli and Esther Béliard, Wébert Lespérance (Boss Pépé), Robert Julien, Georgia Jacques, Jonathas Vil, Paul Vicière,

Pastor Guy Thomas, Micheline Alphonse (Mafi) along with doctors and nurses who played a role in my complete recovery.

To save the best for last, I must say that this book could not have been possible without the One who continues to hold me in His hands of love. At a time when deadly diseases continue to strike young and old, rich and poor at an alarming rate, I give nothing but praise to the One who gave me a second lease of life – a great opportunity to tell the whole world who He really is. Indeed, I have already shared my testimony on a number of radio and TV stations. But as the old dictum states, "words fly away, writings remain."

INTRODUCTION

LIVING THE GOOD LIFE BEFORE FACING HARDSHIP

Over the past three decades in the United States, I have lived quite a productive life. I spent most of my working life in academia. Earning my living for a total of 24 years in the Boston public schools as a language tester, a teaching assistant, and a language teacher, respectively, was a true blessing. Thanks to my advanced degree in math education, I earned the opportunity to quickly move up the social ladder. After struggling to make ends meet holding low-level positions during my first six years in the United States, I had finally experienced the satisfaction of living the American dream.

Apart from being an educator, I co-founded and hosted the first Haitian television show in Boston, *Tele Kreyol*, cablecast on different community access channels across New England, as well as a weekly Haitian radio program, *Echo Evangélique*, the first-ever broadcast on the AM dial in Massachusetts. Developed into a radio station on sub-carrier, *Echo Evangélique* took a big chunk out of my spare time over the last decade, without interfering with my duty of being a devoted father and husband. I took every opportunity to enjoy what I do best in broadcasting: interviewing performing artists, hosting music programs, and producing public service ads (PSAs). Besides hosting a segment about the American government with the station general manager's daughter and another segment on entrepreneurship with my teenage son, I helped create good programming that appealed to our target audience. The amount of support and admiration I gained from my listeners made broadcasting my special enjoyment.

My passion for my local church was also manifest at the helm of its music department. The senior pastor held me in high esteem for being a reliable music director. I always took delight in showing up 30 minutes before Sunday school to make sure all our equipment operated smoothly during worship services. I performed sound checks on our instruments, including keyboards; bass guitar; and my own acoustic guitar, which I considered a second wife, and tested every microphone.

To help the church grow, I also made time to be on the Board of Directors and collaborate with our two pastors and another church member to form a team of facilitators dubbed *the Group of Four*, in charge of leadership development. Having put together a training program for church leaders, we succeeded in providing them the tools necessary to exercise leadership effectively. Through different seminars, our leaders could gain knowledge and experience, in accordance with the church's vision. Because I always challenged myself to use my time efficiently, I could make the most of the moments I had been given to benefit others.

When summer 2014 came, family vacation and outings took priority over my radio and church ministries. Once school was out, my social agenda became quite exciting until the end of August. Besides cooking out and attending weddings with friends and neighbors, my wife, teenage son, and I couldn't wait to travel to Canada and spend quality time with my siblings and other relatives living on the outskirts of Montreal. I refused to miss their great traditional summer barbecue where three generations of the Doutre family get together every July or August to feast not only on burgers, hotdogs, and corn, but also on the best Haitian cuisines such as rice in black mushroom sauce, Macaroni au Gratin, and beet salad.

On that particular July, roughly 75 people, including adults and children, spent hours in the backyard of my sister's mansion where I watched with passion young children frolicking in the swimming pool. Every now and then, they would come around the grill to grab a burger or a hotdog and then splash in the pool with laughter. As for my wife, a photography aficionado, she never got tired of snapping pictures of the entire event with the intent of doing a little showing off at work once we were back from vacation. The Doutre's traditional barbecue would be a conversation piece for her with her colleagues as they detailed how they spent their summer vacations with relatives far away.

I also made plans to travel to Haiti on July 25th and I didn't want to miss that trip for anything, considering how much fun the whole family had the previous year in the countryside. One of my pastors who had built a huge house in his hometown, Fonds-des-Nègres, invited us again to spend part of our summer vacation with him. For my wife, the day of the departure on board American Airlines could not come fast enough. Having landed at 7:00 p.m. at *Aéroport International Toussaint L'Ouverture*, which is three to four hours away from the South, for security reasons, we chose to spend our first night at my sister-in-law's house in Pétionville, not far from the nation's capital. But first thing in the morning, we headed to the South in a friend's SUV.

After two hours of driving we decided to stop at a little restaurant in Miragoâne, the capital of the Nippes Department. The driver, who had Haitian currency available, was kind enough to lend us some money to buy breakfast consisting of spaghetti, chunks of chicken, and other Haitian specialties, which we ate ravenously in the fresh open air. Thirty minutes later, we were back on the road, and by 10:00 a.m., we reached Fonds-des-Nègres. Our beloved host could not have been happier to accommodate us for a week.

Having savored a variety of foods fresh from the trees and enjoyed a beach view complete with a nice breeze and the sound of the ocean in this southern region, I reluctantly returned to Pétionville, under my wife's insistence. She wanted to spend time with her sister and other relatives, so I adhered to her changes in our itinerary. I didn't want to leave the countryside because it was too hot in the western region and I would hardly be able to sleep at night once we arrived. But I found solace in the fact that I could visit the newly renovated *Place Boyer* in Pétionville, where a mysteriously attractive park has been built.

Though traffic was chaotic in Port-au-Prince, three days later I managed to reach *Radio Lumière*, the first American-run radio network where I spent my early broadcasting years as a DJ and then a production director when I was still in high school. During those years, under the moniker Joel Desmornes, I had pioneered and hosted one of the station's most popular daily programs titled *Chan la Kay*, composed of songs from recording groups and artists in Haiti.

Arriving back at the station after three decades, I was really surprised to notice the program still existed under the same title and kept the same time slot: 3:00 p.m. to 4:00 p.m. As a matter of fact, I was a surprise guest on my own show I had created back in 1976. During a live interview with the host, who came from quite a different generation, I was able to talk about the "good ol' days" working at the station as a youth in the late '70s and early '80s.

The station's general manager was so thrilled that he persuaded me to extend my visit for other interviews and photo ops. My family didn't mind spending the extra time with me at the station, but they were not willing to say a single word on the microphone. As I finally decided to head back to Pétionville after those long hours, my teenage son breathed a sigh of relief, saying, "I thought you'd never leave, Dad."

My wife, who clearly understood how much I had wanted to pay a visit to the radio station, asked me, "Are you happy now?"

I told her I had a blast and was looking forward to doing it again the following summer.

At the time, I didn't have a clue as to what was going to happen to me in another month, never mind the following summer. King Solomon says in Proverbs 27:1 that people should not make a noise about tomorrow, for they are not certain what a day's outcome may be. "One Day at a Time," a popular country and western-style Christian song written by Marijohn Wilkin and Kris Kristofferson, has always been one of my favorites. Taking time to reflect on the lyrics helped me become aware of the brevity and uncertainty of life. Also, when I thought about Murphy's Law, which states "anything that can go wrong will go wrong," I was cognizant that a certain class of unwanted events could occur in my life at any moment.

CHAPTER ONE

MY LIFE TAKES A 180• TURN

My normal activities came to a screeching halt in mid-September 2014 when I took a major hit, turning my life upside down. It was not something I had bargained for, knowing how terrific I looked. During social gatherings, some old friends would approach me and say, "Joel, you haven't aged a bit and you look so debonair." Really, I thought I was the picture of good health. This unexpected event arrived at a time when I enjoyed exercise the most. The scorching summer months had passed and I could get up in the morning and spend nearly all day working out. If somebody had asked me if I was healthy, without really understanding what it meant to be in good health, I would have been boasting about my super fitness, not forgetting my perfect diet plan.

Yet, I was hemorrhaging inside, which I didn't become aware of until I went to see my primary care physician (PCP) for an annual physical on September 16, 2014. My blood pressure, 118/70, was in the normal range for a 5' 9" male weighing 172 pounds. The doctor took a chest X-ray and it came back normal.

The day after my physical, however, my PCP called me and urged me to get to the emergency room. When I asked him why, he said, "If you don't go to the ER right now, you might drop dead any minute because your heart doesn't have enough blood to function." He told me that my blood test revealed I was severely anemic; therefore, he begged me to get a blood transfusion as soon as possible to avoid cardiac arrest. My better half, who worked second shift, was not available at the time to take me to the hospital. I didn't go into a panic. Instead of calling the ambulance, I drove myself to the ER.

I remained calm behind the wheel. I didn't let the idea of my heart stopping at any moment take over my thoughts because I had deep roots that could not be moved by circumstances. I was convinced that no matter the outcome, I should be okay and even stronger. Equipped with the power of positivity, I knew everything was happening for a reason. I was sad, indeed, but in the midst of trouble, I relied on the Lord's promises, knowing His love never fails in good days and bad days.

The joy I was experiencing on the road had nothing to do with my unfavorable situation. Besides, I was already acquainted with the notion that joy, a spiritual pleasure, goes against happiness, which simply depends on the circumstances; for example, when I finally secured that teaching position in the Boston public schools with a decent salary attached to it, I was extremely happy, not joyful. Succeeding in getting a job to move upward economically was clearly an outward circumstance. On the other hand, I could be unhappy, yet joyful, at the same time. When my older brother died after a long battle with cirrhosis of the liver, I was heart-broken. Nevertheless, I was clothed with joy, knowing he was in God's presence and no longer had to suffer. Joy is only found in God, as Jeremiah 8:10 says: "Do not grieve, for the joy of the Lord is your strength."

On my arrival to the ER that evening, despite my unhappy circumstance, I was in good spirits. I greeted the receptionist with a big smile and let her know my PCP sent me to the ER for a blood transfusion. It didn't take me long to see the triage nurse, who, after gathering necessary information, determined I should be quickly seen by a doctor. First, the ER doctor performed a rectal exam and smeared a stool sample on a card to test for blood in the stool, which turned positive right away. That was just the tip of the iceberg, however, and before long I would need to brace myself for more serious test results.

A short time later, the nurse, having determined my blood type, received the okay to hook me to an IV pump to replace the lost components of my blood, since my hemoglobin level had already fallen below 10 grams/dL and hematocrit below 20%. Treating this anemia first with a blood transfusion, while I was still waiting to find out the results of the other tests I'd taken, required immediate admission. I had never been hospitalized in my life, but while spending my first night in a hospital, I was comforted by the fact that my soul mate, finally relieved from work, was able to join me in my room. The hospital staff rolled in a folding bed for her, so she didn't have to sleep in a chair after working an eight-hour shift. She vowed to keep me company 24/7 in the hospital and cease her regular activities.

When I woke up the next morning, the love of my life was the first person I saw by my bedside. Then, a group of young physicians in white coats, making their rounds, walked into my room to get acquainted with me. They wanted to know how I had been feeling since the blood transfusion started. After reviewing with me the plan for the day, they quickly moved on to other patients. Minutes later, the gastrointestinal (GI) doctor assigned to diagnose and treat my condition dropped in and announced he was going to run a couple of tests in order to find the real culprit responsible for my blood loss.

Two hours later, at around 9:00 a.m., I was taken to Radiology for an endoscopy. Later on, the result came back normal. Meanwhile, I had to prepare for a colonoscopy, which was certainly a major inconvenience. Getting ready for the procedure took the rest of the day and most of the night. The purgative part, consisting of taking a powerful bowel-clearing substance and coping with the resulting diarrhea, was no pleasure, but the colonoscopy, which was performed the following day, allowed the GI doctor to find the perpetrator: my large intestine.

Soon after the procedure, the GI doctor came out and bluntly informed me, "This is not good news,

Mr. Doutre. We need to have a serious talk. It looks like you've been having this problem for more than a year and you need aggressive treatments as soon as possible."

For some reason, I didn't have any mind-boggling reaction to this terrible diagnosis. Psalm 112:7 says, "He is not afraid of bad news; his heart is firm, trusting in the Lord."

More bad news arrived on the third day of my stay in the hospital. A CT scan and an MRI revealed I had cancer that had metastasized to my lymph nodes, adrenaline glands, and liver. I didn't freak out, however, because I knew Jesus could cure any disease, no matter how chronic. During His ministry on earth, Jesus healed people with all kinds of diseases. He healed the ten lepers and the woman "with an issue of blood and other variants" for 12 years. I knew Jesus had not changed because Hebrews 13:8 says He is the same yesterday, today, and forever. He calls Himself the Alpha and the Omega three times in the book of Revelation (Revelation 1:8 and 21:6, 13). He was the fourth man walking in the fire with Shadrach, Meshach, and Abednego, the three Jewish youths who had professed their faith in God to King Nebuchadnezzar before they were thrown into the fiery furnace. They said in Daniel 3:17-18:

If we are thrown into the blazing fire, the God we serve is able to deliver us from it, and He will deliver us from Your Majesty's hand. But even if He does not, we want you to know, Your Majesty, that we will not serve your gods or worship the image golden you have set up.

If the three young men didn't die in the flames because of the presence of the Lord who met them in the furnace, I was confident that Jesus was walking with me when the flames of cancer were rising around me, threatening to destroy my life. I didn't hesitate to tell my doctors, therefore, that I had no fear because battling cancer was not my fight. The faith I had in God at the time made me braver than I had ever been.

In the hospital, I could remember God's message to King Jehoshaphat through Prophet Jahaziel in 2 Chronicles 20:15: "Be not afraid nor dismayed by reason of this great multitude; for the battle is not yours, but God's." This passage made me understand it was not in my own strength I was going to fight my enemy. To expect victory and deliverance, trusting God to vanquish this deadly disease was a must and I had no reason to be terrified. I was determined to carry on regardless of how advanced the cancer was because it could not tear down my faith in the Lord.

CHAPTER TWO

GETTING READY FOR THE FIRST BATTLE

Upon my release from the hospital a week later, I went back to my regular routine. The fact that I had a cancerous colon that needed aggressive care didn't prevent me from living my daily life. With my hemoglobin level up to 13.5 grams/dL and my hematocrit level up to 30%, my heart had enough blood to function. Since the lab test done before I left the hospital showed I was still anemic, I was advised not to go overboard. The slow bleeding within my large intestine, which could not be stopped without an operation, prompted the GI doctor to prescribe a 325mg daily dose of ferrous sulfate while I awaited surgery. In addition, the nutrition nurse recommended an iron regimen consisting of foods such as spinach, eggs, pumpkin seeds, and nuts, designed to enhance the absorption of iron into my system.

To be honest, I was no stranger to this kind of diet. In fact, over the last 10 years, I had been fascinated with broccoli, kale, and spinach, which I thought would keep me from being *sick*. As for eggs, I never paid attention to dietary naysayers who decided that cholesterol in eggs translated into artery-clogging cholesterol in the blood. At least twice a week for breakfast, I would eat scrambled or boiled eggs, credited with having a high nutritional value. Pumpkin seeds and nuts could always be found on top of my fridge. So getting the right diet to boost my iron level was not the real issue here.

Getting the right surgeon to remove my cancer was my main concern. I was quite skittish about the hospital my insurance had selected for me to undergo the surgery. I'd heard some negative reports from patients who had bad experiences with that medical institution. One of the victims was my pastor's wife, whose intestine was punctured by mistake during an operation. Nevertheless, I found solace when my PCP assured me that my surgeon was considered one of the best in the practice. He told me I should be worry-free.

Effectively, when my wife and I sat in the surgeon's office to discuss the procedure and express our concerns and fears, we thought he was very impressive. The surgeon graphically showed us on map of the human body the diseased portions of the colon to be removed, which he estimated to weigh four pounds. "No big deal," he said. "It will be a minimally invasive surgery done through a small incision with a small camera, and the operation will last only two hours. You will need no colostomy bag. Except for complications, which are unlikely to occur, you will spend three days in the hospital following the operation, and after two weeks, you'll be able to go back to teaching. My secretary already booked you for Wednesday, October 8th, at 12 p.m. If you are not ready, we can change the date."

I took my surgeon at face value. I told him if that was the case, I couldn't wait to get that tumor out of me. My wife was very supportive of my decision to have the surgery done as soon as possible. She always saw me as a strong husband who would not back down in the face of adversity. Wholeheartedly, when I left the surgeon's office I felt relieved, without a second thought about having the operation.

I was in such good spirits that I continued to attend all sorts of church activities: prayer meetings, Bible studies, Sunday services, and so forth. Three days before the surgery, I spoke at a church family night event on the topic "Relationship Between Parents and Children: Cultural Conflict," a prevalent issue among Haitians living in the Diaspora. Though battling cancer, God's Spirit living inside me allowed me to engage everybody's attention like I had never done before. After giving a general overview of three parenting styles – authoritarian, authoritative, and permissive – I asked the question, "Where exactly do Haitian parents fit?"

A good number of youngsters didn't hesitate to admit that their parents apply the authoritarian style, which the kids found too dictatorial. This was a good opportunity for parents and youths alike to voice their concerns and share their different points of view. On that Sunday evening, the families were so into the discussion they made me forget I was living with a serious illness. I also had no idea this was going to be my last speaking engagement for a very long time. It was truly a fun moment filled with music, jokes, and foods. I had no reservation whatsoever in terms of interacting with different families gathering in the church basement. The word "operation" did not come to my mind at all. Spiritually, morally, and mentally, I felt very strong, being surrounded by people who thought the world of me. Above all, God's grace resided upon me.

On the eve of my surgery, the senior pastor and a few elders came to my house in the morning to offer spiritual support. They stayed a little while to chat first with the family, then sang a few songs, read a couple Psalms of supplication, and prayed for God's intervention, in light of what James 5:14-16 says:

Is anyone among you sick? Let them call the elders of the church to pray over them and anoint them with oil in the name of the Lord. And the prayer offered in faith will make the sick person well; the Lord will raise them up. If they have sinned, they will be forgiven. Therefore confess your sins to each other and pray for each other so that you may be healed. The prayer of a righteous person is powerful and effective.

In my mind, God was going to exercise His grace upon me and I didn't have to go through surgery. My faith was based on what the Lord had done years ago for one of the church leaders who had been diagnosed with colorectal cancer before he became a Christian. In a vision while resting in bed, he heard a voice saying, "I am going to change your cancer into hemorrhoids." Instantly, that man who was about to have a major surgery turned and looked around to see if there was someone else in the room. It took him a little while to realize he was in the room alone.

Before going under the knife, he asked his GI doctor to perform a last exam. To the physician's surprise, the result showed no trace of cancer, except some hemorrhoids lurking in his rectum, as the voice had spoken before. Psalm 147:15 says, "When God sends his command to the earth, his word runs swiftly."

Based on that earlier event, I had just assumed God would do the same for me. But I forgot that God was sovereign in the exercise of His grace and that His power is exercised as He wills and when He wills. As David says in Psalm 115:3, "Our God is in Heaven; He does whatever He pleases." Who am I to tell God when I expect my miracle? In prayer I was asking God for a quick fix, which was not in His plan. Sometimes, it is important to wait on the Lord when going through adversity. While waiting, I petitioned the Lord to reveal Himself to me in His own way.

The night before the operation, one of the church deacons called me on the phone to let me know I needed to be strong. He didn't hesitate to relay

God's message to me: "Tell Brother Joel he is going to fight for his life in the hospital." When I informed him that my surgeon had already given me a different perspective while sitting in his office to discuss the procedure, he told me like a prophet that God had spoken, and therefore I should be bracing for a serious battle.

Instead of going hysterical, I spent part of the evening reflecting on Psalm 23, which provided me words of comfort in that difficult moment. If the Lord is my shepherd, I should not be afraid of anything. Indeed, I was diagnosed with an advanced cancer. But God didn't tell me I was going to die; He told me I was going to fight for my life. As Jesus laid down His life for me, He would not let me fall off the cliff. For a moment I thought God might allow me to have a near-death experience, but I firmly believed I would pull through God's way, not the doctors' way. Having acknowledged God's sovereignty over my life through Psalm 23, I went to bed in peace and slept through the night.

I woke up in the morning, rejuvenated. For a person who was about to undergo surgery for the first time, I didn't feel terrified at all. Calmly, I asked my wife to sign the health care proxy form before heading to the hospital. She started crying and wanted to know why she was signing that form. "Are you going to die, honey?" she asked. I told her not to worry. I assured her it was just a form giving her the authority to make health care decisions for me should I become incapacitated. A few minutes later, Sister Jacky, a church member, showed up. The three of us prayed together and by 9:00 a.m., we hit the road to the hospital.

CHAPTER THREE

MY HEALTH TURNING INTO CHAOS

On October 8, 2014, around 11:00 a.m., I was lying in a small bed in a surgical prep area. Frightened? No. I felt the presence of the Lord had already surrounded me by the time the pre-operative nurse came to complete my medical history and assessment, provide pre-op instructions and education, start an intravenous line, and oversee the pre-op preparation my surgeon had requested. It was a long wait. The time spent waiting in the prep area alone was so long that for a minute I thought the staff overseeing and performing my surgery had all forgotten about me.

Finally, around 1:00, the nurse came back to the room and apologized for the delay. She informed me that an emergency operation was afoot and that I needed to wait at least another hour. In the meantime, my wife went to the cafeteria to grab something to eat. When she returned at 2:00, I was still alone waiting for the anesthesiologist, who didn't show up until 2:30. He was apologetic and tried to put me at ease by cracking a few jokes before administering the anesthesia. At 2:45, I was finally taken to the operating room and I remained asleep for the duration of the procedure.

I could not believe how well I felt when I woke up in the recovery room. I overheard someone saying, "This guy is a real fighter." The surgeon approached me to congratulate me on being one of his best patients in the OR that day. Sister Jacky, who had been keeping my wife company since morning, told me I didn't look like someone who just had surgery. My siblings and other relatives who had arrived from Canada also paid me an enormous compliment on how well I looked after the operation. My curious baby sister asked me to show her the incision site and she was pleased when she saw just a little piece of gauze on my abdomen. Apparently, I was genuinely repaired and ready to leave the hospital in three days or less, from the surgical team's point of view.

The doctors' plan, however, didn't work out exactly the way they thought it would. One day after the operation, I began developing post-operative complications, including abdominal pain, high fever, chills, and aspiration pneumonia. One of the nurses told me the aspiration pneumonia was not a post-surgery-related infection, according to the doctors. She tried to convince me it was something I started developing days before the operation. The surgical team came around and asked me all sorts of questions about my health history. Namely, they wanted to know if I was an alcoholic, an IV drug user, or a cigarette smoker, but none of these epithets applied to me. I had the feeling a surgical error was made and nobody wanted to come clean. In the meantime, I was on antibiotics and oxygen, hoping the infection and my breathing difficulties would go away.

Two days later, my hands started shaking. When the nurse asked me if I was feeling cold, I told her it was more than that. She thought it was simply a side effect of the medications, but I didn't want to take that at face value. I begged her to call the doctor right away and she immediately ran to the phone. Soon, my whole body went into a convulsion. In less than five minutes, the doctor rushed to the room and hooked me to a blood pressure machine. I could read the monitor where my blood pressure jumped from 150/70 to 300/150. My heart was beating so fast I saw death flashing right before my eyes. In one minute, an EKG was performed and the doctor injected me with something that stopped the convulsion and normalized my blood pressure to 140/70.

A CT scan of my chest, abdomen, and pelvis the following day revealed a major mistake was made during the operation. Unbelievably, the surgical team failed to re-join the small bowel to the large bowel. They all went into a panic when they realized what their surgical error had caused – pulmonary infection, as well as kidney and heart failure. The highest incidence of post-surgical complications occurred early on Sunday around 2:00 a.m. when I went into septic shock, which forced the doctors to transfer me to the intensive care unit (ICU). The undesirable decision they made to put me in a medically induced coma in an attempt to save my life required my wife's permission. Having seen on the table the giant needle ready to go through my neck, she burst into tears while signing the authorization form because she felt she was signing my death warrant. At least the doctors in the ICU were honest and told her they were going to take a big risk with no guarantee they would succeed.

That Sunday morning, the day I fell into a coma, I didn't even have a chance to say goodbye to my siblings and other relatives who had to hit the road back to Montreal because of their jobs. I learned from my wife that they were in tears when they saw me breathing through machines, with my tongue sticking out. The ICU nurse, in an attempt to comfort everybody, invited them to take turns whispering something in my ear. "Maybe he'll be able to hear you," she said. Too bad, I couldn't hear a thing. They left in despair, not certain they would see me alive again.

In the early afternoon on Sunday the 12th, the surgeon had to leave home on his day off to join the surgical team to perform an emergency operation on me while I was in a coma because it was the only way they could fix their mistake. After the procedure was over, they had to leave me in the recovery room overnight, with the incision wide open; the doctors found it too dangerous to sew me back up because they thought I could get infected again. They had to cover the entire wound area with a piece of foam to apply what is called "vacuum-assisted closure."

This time, I ended up with a double-barrel colostomy, dividing the colon into two ends that formed separate stomas. Stools exited from one of the stomas. Mucus made by the colon exited from the other.

As days went by, I remained in a coma. My inability to come out of it puzzled and frightened all the physicians trying desperately to treat my condition, according to my wife. As she kept begging them to find a way to save my life, those doctors were forthright enough to admit there was nothing they could do in their own power to change the situation. My wife just had to pray and wait for a miracle. Battling cancer in front of her was one thing. But my dying from post-surgical complications was not something she was ready to handle.

A couple of haters posing as friends came in for a short visit, as I learned from a credible source. As bad news traveled fast, those adversaries didn't waste time rushing to the hospital. They just wanted to confirm what they had heard about my imminent death before they proceeded with their little celebration. But people who had always appreciated me through my radio and church ministries also stopped by in small groups to pray for the best when doctors expected the worst.

My pastor, who was very supportive at all levels, came to the hospital every day, in spite of his busy schedule. He didn't take my situation lightly. He not only called members of his congregation, urging them to throw their support behind my wife, who needed all kinds of help, but he also kept sending text messages to his fellow ministers, urging them to pray for my recovery. In response, other ministers from the Church of the Nazarene in the New England district showed up, petitioning God for a miracle. Those who habitually looked at me with amazement as I jumped around with my guitar during church revivals were in dismay when they saw me fighting for my life, machines beeping away, and tubes everywhere. Even in this condition, any pastor could have access to my room because my wife told the hospital staff it was okay to let people come to pray as long as visiting hours permitted.

Meanwhile, the news spread through different social media outlets and, in no time, Boston, New York, Miami, Montreal, Haiti, and other cities around the world were holding special prayer meetings, asking the Redeemer to intercede on my behalf. There is no distance between God and us in prayer because we serve a God who transcends time and space. His ubiquitous influence, as my family members believed, could make an impact as I was trapped between life and death in a hospital.

Still, I remained comatose and my situation was considered irreversible. Even still, my wife was hopeful. But the moment came when she was told to prepare for the worst. So, she went home with tears in her eyes and in despair announced to her mother, "I don't think Joel is coming back home." She thought she would have to start planning my funeral real soon.

CHAPTER FOUR

WHAT TO EXPECT IN THE WORST OF TIMES

My church congregation was recovering emotionally from the death of a husband and wife couple, each of whom died unexpectedly, two months apart. My pastor was called to officiate a third funeral service three months later, which he would have found very difficult to do. So, desperately, he texted the congregation and asked all the members to come to the church for an urgent prayer session. While the devoted members did not ignore the pastor's request since they truly believe in the power of prayer in the midst of a crisis, they were also acquainted with the Biblical notion that "God does whatever He pleases."

So that evening, the pastor began by addressing the assembly with this remark: "Maybe it's time for Brother Joel to go home to be with the Lord.

But we are going to ask God for an extension." Before all the members started praying, they read in unison 2 Kings 20, where God extended the life of Hezekiah, the 13th king of Judah, after he became deathly ill. At the end of the prayer meeting, the pastor asked the congregation to "leave everything up to God who always decides what's best for His servant."

The Lord decided to intervene His way without being pushed around. At the same time, however, God didn't want anybody to feel their prayers went unanswered. I believe every prayer directed to God in my favor from the beginning of my ordeal was stored away and came to fruition at a later date, according to His plan. As King David says to the Almighty in Psalm 56:8, "You have kept count of my wanderings; store my tears in your water-skin – aren't they already recorded in your book?"

While I was in the coma, I saw the glory of the Lord, and I felt so good that I didn't want to wake up. I felt just as Paul did in Philippians 1:23, "I desire to depart and be with Christ, which is better by far." I wonder how Lazarus felt before Jesus raised him from the dead.

At the appointed time, after a week in a coma, however, I awoke to the doctors' amazement. In the process of waking up, I had a sort of veil attached to both eyes and I could barely see my friends who came to pay me a visit. One by one, they felt it necessary to come close to my face to say hi. It was like seeing them through a magnifying glass; their faces looked gigantic and I saw their gigantic smiles, as well. They were elated to see another Lazarus coming back from the dead.

When I was fully awake, I was in shock when I realized I was hooked to different machines. So, I started swinging my arms and pulling at the tubes that were sunk into my nostrils. Trained medical staff had my hands tied to stop the madness. I became so agitated that the physician in charge injected me with anesthetic, which put me to sleep.

When I awoke once again, I realized my wife had been singing in my ear a very popular Haitian church song, *Bondye fidèl e li pote fado-m yo. Li seche dlo nan je-m…* (God is faithful and lifted all my burdens. He wiped away my tears…). When she came close to me, she gave me a gentle kiss. In return, I gave her a gentle smile, a smile she had not seen in a long time. She said, "Thank you, honey, for coming back for me." For several reasons, I guess it was in God's will that I live in the flesh again. As Paul says in Philippians 1:22, "If I am to go on living in the body, this will mean fruitful labor for me."

The same week in the ICU, my wife witnessed another miracle unfolding. Previously, during my pelvic exam, a mass had been discovered in my bladder, causing me extreme pain. Usually, this kind of case requires surgery to remove the mass. God knew I could not afford to go through a third operation. Suddenly, my wife saw a kind of white powder cruising through the catheter tube to the drain bag. When she pushed the emergency button, on-duty medical staff intervened immediately and they could not explain what really happened. I believe God was still at work during those difficult moments.

Meanwhile, I could barely talk. I had problems communicating with the medical staff, and even my wife, who had known me for 22 years. Since I hadn't brushed my teeth in three weeks, I had layers of white stuff stuck to my tongue. My mouth felt so uncomfortable that I tried several times to get my wife to clean it up, but she could not understand what I was trying to tell her. Finally, she grabbed a piece of paper and a pen and gave it to me so I could write down my request. But my hand was so shaky that I could not even scribble the words "brush my teeth." She asked me to give it another try, and this time she was able to decipher my crooked penmanship. Unfortunately, once the toothbrush touched my tongue, I started screaming in pain because my tongue was too sensitive to handle the cleaning. I just had to be satisfied with the oral sponge swab the nurse occasionally put in my mouth to keep it moist.

The coma left me with some side effects in the groin area. As a result of prolonged time stuck in bed, the scrotal skin had peeled off and topical treatments seemed unsuccessful. My wife, who didn't want my scrotum to deteriorate, was begging the doctors and nurses to come up with a better treatment. I became so needy that my wife had to petition the night shift nurse to let her stay in the ICU so she could keep an eye on me. The medical staff granted her permission to stay with me every night, sitting on a hard chair close to my bed.

On one particular night when I needed her the most, however, one of the nurses gently kicked her out of the room at 2:00 a.m. "You look tired, Mrs. Doutre," she said. "Maybe it's time for you to go home to get some sleep." Unfortunately, everybody seemed relieved to get rid of her because she kept asking too many questions and stopping doctors from giving me certain medications she thought were too risky, owing to her basic knowledge and experience in physical and mental health. So, I was saddened when I couldn't find her in the room to help me that night.

When she came back in the afternoon, she told me she had to sit in the main lobby from 2:00 a.m. to 7:00 a.m. and wait for the ticket booth window to open so she could get her car from the parking lot. Ever since then, she vowed to leave the hospital no later than 8:00 p.m. when visiting hours were over. When she wasn't around at night, I had to deal with the reality that someone would take forever to show up when I pressed the nurse's call button.

In the ICU, I was still fighting a high-grade fever because the intestine had perforated, which caused its contents to leak into my abdomen. To alleviate the fever, nurses coalesced around the idea of keeping the room cold at all times. Being in a cold room and coping with a high fever at the same time could be exasperating. On one particular night, it became so unbearable that I started shivering and coughing. Though I was struggling with verbal communication, I managed to petition a third shift nurse (who was probably in her 70s) to turn up the heat. She turned down my request, saying, "It's already midnight and no patient needs heat at this time." Then she disappeared because she didn't want to be bothered. Meanwhile, I kept coughing profusely.

Later on, I managed to splash the bed and the wall near me with significant amounts of phlegm. In order to find some relief, I pressed the nurse's call button again. When she showed up this time, she looked a little grouchy. Seeing mucus all over the place, she became upset with me and made this remark: "Oh my God! It only takes one night for one patient to mess up the wonderful work I have been doing for this hospital for 30 years."

To calm her down, I gently told her I had been an educator for 24 years, and my students always came first regardless of their behavior in my classroom; it was still my responsibility to serve their best interests.

She simply replied, "Ooh, you're a teacher!" Right there, I sensed some sarcasm from her response – a euphemism for "big whoop!" Anyway, I took solace in knowing that my situation in the hospital would not last forever.

After a sleepless night, at 7:00 a.m. sharp, transport came to wheel me to Interventional Radiology (IR) for a pelvic drain. The doctor doing the procedure worked very hard to locate the problem, but to his surprise he couldn't find any fluid. Apparently, by the time I was taken to IR, all fluids and fever had vanished overnight. After the radiologist monitored me for two hours, he finally called transport to take me back to the ICU.

Having found no further reason to keep me in the ICU, my doctors decided to transfer me to a general ward in the hospital that same morning. When I got there, I found myself in a room that looked like a hotel suite only a CEO could afford. It was a spacious room equipped with nice furniture and comfortable chairs for visitors, a fridge to keep my perishables, and an extra bed to accommodate my wife without her needing to go home to rest and sleep. It was a dream come true; she could now keep me company 24/7 in the hospital, and I could not wait for her to come back to find that out.

In the meantime, I was tired of getting a clear liquid diet consisting mostly of chicken broth, cranberry juice, and jello desserts, three times a day. After taking two sips, I would leave everything on the tray for the trash. Lord, have mercy! I was yearning for real food, but I was having difficulty verbalizing that desire. Finally, one of the physical therapists, who had finally decided to transfer me to a recliner, started cautiously feeding me some Graham crackers and cranberry juice, testing my readiness for solid foods. As those crackers went down my throat with no problem, I asked her for more. Not only was my PT compliant, but she also shared with me the good news that, as of lunch time, the doctor would send in an order for the food service to put me on a regular diet. I felt like a baby reaching a new milestone, transitioning from clear liquid to solid foods. Even though as a grown man, I have a refined palate for foods, I still enjoyed those crackers as I waited for a hot meal.

My pastor, who had just arrived on the scene was so amazed with the new situation that he began shouting "Hallelujah! Praise the Lord!" Even though he was in a "hush area" of the hospital, he could not quiet himself when he witnessed such a turn of events happening so soon. Immediately, on his cell phone, he called my wife, who was sleeping at home. She ignored the call, however, since she was very tired.

My pastor tried to reach her a second time. Reluctantly, she answered the phone and heard the pastor say, "Sister Carine, I want to let you talk to someone." When he passed the phone to me, I told her the PT had decided to let me sit in a chair so I could eat some crackers. Immediately, she jumped out of her bed and headed to the shower. In record time, she made it to the hospital and saw the new me (a newly reborn me, I would say) sitting in a chair, smiling and waiting for lunch to be served. The moment she arrived, I called food service to order lunch for her, as a free guest tray per patient, per meal, was allowed.

With such a big improvement, I started thinking about my church revival I was going to miss for the first time. Looking back at those past joyful events loaded with praise songs and music, my desire to be there to play music was a Holy Grail. Even for a moment, my wife entertained the crazy thought of asking my doctor if she could take me to the church revival and drive me back to the hospital every night. She wouldn't be able to do that by a long shot, however, and I had to accept the fact that the revival would go on without me this time. I wished I could have at least watched the services on TV, but the church could not provide the live coverage. So I just had to wait for the following year's revival.

CHAPTER FIVE

TRANSITIONING FROM THE HOSPITAL

As I was making impressive strides, the hospital staff decided to send me home. But my wife, who thought I was not in good enough shape to return home without physical and occupational therapy, rebuked the staff's decision. She was spearheading the effort to have me placed in a rehab center to get the service I needed before I went back home. When she contacted the medical social worker, however, she found out our health insurance would not pay for rehab. My wife, who never takes no for an answer, was all over the place playing advocate, protector, guardian, and so on. She was fighting tooth and nail to have my transition to a rehab facility approved.

At a certain point, she could no longer fight, however, because her body could not take it anymore. So, she took a break from my cause and went home to rest. But what little physical strength she had left took its final toll on her, and she had to call one of her sorority sisters to rush her to the emergency room. Suffering from extreme exhaustion combined with a chronic fever, my wife was admitted to a hospital nearby – the last thing I was expecting. Heartbroken by the situation, I felt as if I had no one left to lead the fight for me.

Every time a nurse stopped by my room, I whined like a little boy who wanted his mommy, complaining about how devastated I was over my wife's hospitalization. Once I began reflecting on Job's adverse situation, however, I realized it was time for me to suck it up and act like a man. God never told me the road to victory would be easy. True, I missed her because she was my lifeline, but I had no reason to be discouraged by her absence when God was working out my problems behind the scenes, only I hadn't realized it yet.

As days passed by, my wife recovered and regained her strength. As soon as she was released from the hospital, she rejoined me at my bed side and the fight with the insurance company to cover the cost for my rehab resumed.

Meanwhile, my wife was searching for the best and most suitable rehab facility. Finally, the insurance company approved my move to a rehab center.

For some reason, however, the medical social worker in charge of my paperwork, was dragging her feet. She kept saying, "I have a heavy caseload of patients on my back and your husband is next on my list." When my wife called the insurance company to voice her concern about the delay, she was told that someone on the hospital staff just had to sign off on the transfer because everything had been taken care of already. When she returned to the medical social worker's office, everything was settled.

On Election Day, November 4, 2014, I was on my way to rehab. My wife, traveling in her own car behind the ambulance, got lost in traffic. When she realized she was following the wrong wagon with a different patient on board, she said to herself, "Wait a minute! This is not my husband. This guy is white and he is not lying down." She had the correct address, however, so she drove straight to the rehab facility and even arrived ahead of me. In fact, she had to wait at the front desk for a good half hour before my ambulance finally arrived. When she asked the driver and the paramedic what took them so long, they said, "We got lost." She was not exasperated over the delay; she was just thankful they had brought me there.

For the first time, I was going to experience life in a nursing home. True, I was not placed on the same floor with patients who were going to be there long-term, but I had assumed the staffing would be minimal in order to reduce costs. One thing I knew for sure: this new environment was going to begin a new chapter on my road to recovery.

My first supper that evening made me feel closer to home. Relishing a hot meal in Haitian culinary style, while watching the CNN midterm election results across the country, already gave me the impression that life in the nursing home wouldn't be that bad. Following supper, I switched to a local channel showing Martha Coakley and Charlie Baker running neck and neck in the exit poll for the Massachusetts Governor race. It didn't take me long to fall asleep. The night shift nurse gently woke me up around 1:00 to empty my colostomy bag, telling me she didn't want my bed to get messy on my first night. When I asked her, "What about other nights?" she promised me she would do her best to take care of my needs. That was good enough for me and I went back to sleep.

First thing the next morning, one of the therapists came to my room for a short meeting to explain the kinds of exercises I should expect to be doing in occupational therapy. She told me the exercises would be designed to rebuild my strength and get me back on my feet. She returned three hours later, around 10:00, to get me to the gym to start physical therapy, but I was having trouble moving around. She realized my abdominal muscles had atrophied a great deal as a result of the open surgery, so she deemed it more appropriate to begin with gentle exercises in my room instead, without straining my abdominal muscles or posing harm to my wound.

The next day, she was poised to take me to the gym on the third floor, but the only way she could do that was to put me in a wheelchair and ride me up the elevator. Once I got to the gym, I managed to move to an exercise bike to do some foot work, designed to improve blood flow in my legs, and other exercises to facilitate healing and reduce muscle spasms. I had to take it slow the first time, but day by day I was gaining confidence in the gym. To be honest, there were days I was tempted to stay in bed without trying to exercise, and sometimes, after the morning session with the PT, I felt like skipping the afternoon session with the OT. But my therapists were great motivators. Having realized what I was in for, I was determined to gain strength and get moving again in record time.

Meanwhile, I was coping with a substantially large wound on my belly, tied to a wound V.A.C. machine. Occasionally, the wound care nurse had to intervene because of continuous problems with the V.A.C. beeping and the dressing losing suction pressure. Fortunately, there was a number on the machine she could call to troubleshoot the problems. But one time the beeping sound refused to go away, despite the collective efforts by the wound care nurse and the support technician on the phone. After countless unsuccessful attempts to fix the problem, the technician finally admitted the wound V.A.C. machine needed to be replaced. So, I had to spend a sleepless night with the nagging beeping noise, while waiting for the company to ship a new machine overnight.

I was also dealing with a double-barrel colostomy. The bag attached to the stoma oozing mucus didn't require that much care, but the bag collecting feces from the other stoma had to be emptied every three hours and changed every two days. When the charge nurse could not carry out this task on a regular basis because of her heavy case load, the colostomy pouch filled with stool, and gas sometimes caused the bag to burst. Believe me, bag blowout is no fun. Every time the bag ballooned overnight, I woke up in a mess, which sometimes meant I had to delay my breakfast. The morning nurse, who had to clean me up and change not only the bed but my colostomy bag, as well, was not a happy camper, especially when she had to run to needy patients who kept screaming for attention.

On the mornings I had doctors' appointments, however, the first shift nurse found a way to come to my room and give me the assistance I needed on time before the ambulance arrived to transport me to the hospital. I guess nobody wanted to be held accountable for me missing medical appointments. There would be no excuse since the rehab facility had all the scheduled appointments for each patient on file. Besides, the doctor's office would call at least 24 hours in advance to remind the staff of my appointments. Thankfully, I was always picked up an hour before the appointment so I could arrive at the hospital on time, even with traffic.

Since I had reached some degree of immobility, the use of a wheelchair became necessary for me to move around the doctor's office. Even though I had become temporarily disabled, I rested in the fact that I would see light at the end of the tunnel, as David says in Psalm 30:5: "Weeping may stay for the night, but rejoicing comes in the morning." Soon, my surgeon realized the post-surgery wound on my belly was healing fast and I didn't have to be tied up to that machine too much longer. He promised to cut me loose on my next appointment. On my last meeting, as my wound had almost completely healed, my surgeon moved to unplug the machine to give me the ability to move around freely once again.

Getting rid of the wound V.A.C. machine allowed me to reach a new step on my journey to recovery. I didn't have to depend on the medical staff as much anymore. I was able to walk to the bathroom to brush my teeth, take a bath, and empty my colostomy bag myself. But I still needed the staff's assistance to change the bag and clean up the stoma giving out stool. On a few occasions, I was given the opportunity to complete this delicate task under a nurse's supervision.

I was also making considerable strides in the gym. Session after session, my muscles were continuously strengthening, and I was completing all the exercise requirements faster than my therapists could imagine. Within two weeks, I switched from a wheelchair to a walker, then from a walker to a cane, and finally I was able to walk without an assistive device. Since I was able to stroll around, my OT invited me to the kitchen to bake some sugar-free brownies, which turned out to be my last assignment in therapy. By November 20th, my discharge papers were ready and I couldn't wait to be home, sweet home.

CHAPTER SIX

MY FIRST BREAK FROM HARDSHIP

As the saying goes, there is no place like home. After being away for a month and a half, what could be better than eating a home-cooked meal in the company of beloved family members, not to forget sharing the same bed with my wife? For hours after my return home, my wife and I kept reflecting on the fragility of life. With no guarantee how many years we would have to share in this life, we both acknowledged that we ought to cherish each other day by day.

My wife could remember the day I was hanging by a thread following a surgery that was supposed to require only a 48-hour hospitalization. But even though I found myself in a situation that looked like the point of no return, God was in control. And we know that "all things work together for the good of those who love God and those who have been called according to His purpose." (Romans 8:28)

Two days after my release from the hospital, the pastor and his associate showed up at our home for a visit. Since my wife and I considered them family members, my wife invited them to my bedroom where I was resting comfortably. The minute they saw me, they looked thrilled. As they were filled with amazement, they told me nobody could have ever foreseen such a miraculous recovery.

After chatting with me briefly, the two pastors, through songs and prayer, thanked the Lord for His divine intervention. During that moment, I echoed what David says in Psalm 116:12: "What shall I render to the Lord for all His benefits toward me?" Like David, I was determined to pay my vows unto the Lord in front of His people at church, which I called my second home. I let the pastors know, therefore, that I could not wait for Sunday because I had an urge to attend the worship service.

Quickly, the senior pastor replied, "I don't think it's a good idea right now, Brother Joe, because you need time to rest and recuperate before you go back to church." He convinced me to wait for the following Sunday, November 30th, to give him time to prepare a Thanksgiving service to celebrate my return with trumpets and fanfare. Reluctantly, I agreed to follow my pastor's advice, but I was hoping he would change his mind.

After the two pastors left, I told my wife I did not want to skip church and that I would not feel comfortable staying home.

Two hours later, the senior pastor called me on the phone and said, "Brother Joe, who am I to stop you from coming to church as soon as you want to praise God? If you want to be in attendance tomorrow, please feel free to do so. But don't tell anybody because I need your return to be a surprise for the congregation." He instructed me to arrive in the parking lot not before 11:00 a.m. and sit in the back of the church where not too many people would notice me. Believe me, I was on cloud nine, knowing how much I missed church.

As soon as I got off the phone, I went straight to my wardrobe to see if I could find a suit that would fit me, as I had lost so much weight due to the cancer. In less than two months, I went from 172 pounds to 143. Since all my clothes were way too big on me, the next morning I decided to borrow an outfit from my teenage son.

As my wife and I walked into the church building that Sunday while the worship service was already in progress, a few people sitting in the back thought they had seen a ghost. After all, they remembered when I was deathly ill, so they never would have believed I could be back on my feet and in church so quickly. As I sat quietly in the pew that morning, I overheard someone near me whispering, "No way. It's not Brother Joel. That's impossible." I kept quiet because I didn't want people to notice me too soon.

Later on, during the announcements, the pastor asked the congregation to stand up and give thanks to God "for Brother Joel's return from the hospital." Those who didn't see me entering the building thought I was home recuperating. But when he invited me to speak for a few minutes, it was like an earthquake. People were crying, clapping, jumping out of their seats, and saying "Alleluia, *Beniswa Letènel* (Praise be to God)." I was all choked up before I could start speaking.

I began my five-minute speech with Psalm 118:17: "I shall not die, but live, and declare the works of the Lord." I cheerfully assured the congregation that my time to die had not yet come, according to God's plan. Not to boast, I told them my sickness was not unto death, but unto the glory of God.

My wife, who had been always been shy in public, took the microphone at the pastor's invitation and spoke with confidence. Standing before the pulpit, she exuded an undeniable joy, praising the Lord for His faithfulness. In record time, she managed to summarize my 45-day ordeal in the hospital and in rehab. Believe me, my wife was a better communicator than I was that Sunday. She closed her testimony with a sense of purpose, expressing the desire to be closer to God in return for all the incredible things the Lord had done for her husband. Our personal testimony was just the tip of the iceberg; a Thanksgiving celebration, intended to mark my triumphant return, was scheduled for the following Sunday.

On Sunday, November 30th, friends from the media and other churches joined our congregation for a glorious event. As testifying to God's faithfulness called for celebration, a worship team, specially selected for the occasion, led the assembly with traditional and contemporary Christian songs such as "How Great Thou Art," "Here I Am to Worship,"

"Lord, I Lift Your Name on High," "He's a Wonderful Savior to Me," and "Jesus is Always There." Other talented performing artists were also invited to be part of the event. The songs they performed were specially selected from their repertoire and really reflected the occasion.

For the first time since October 5, 2014, I was able to pull my acoustic guitar from its case and play along with the other musicians, without rehearsing in advance. When my pastor told me he didn't expect me to play so soon, I let him know I could not wait to return to my music ministry. Besides, God had provided me with enough strength and muscle, so why not join the praise with my own instrument?

As the time allocated for testimonies came, the assembly could not wait to hear what I, the living proof of miracles, had to say. I opened my testimony with Psalm 91:14-16: "'Because he loves me,' says the LORD, 'I will rescue him; I will protect him, for he acknowledges my name. He will call on me, and I will answer him; I will be with him in trouble, I will deliver him and honor him. With long life I will satisfy him and show him my salvation.'" For a while, I shared with people my horrific experience in the hospital and the way God intervened to save my life. I took time to recount all the complications I had endured because of the doctors' mistakes that had nearly driven me to death. I promised them I would devote myself to God's ministry.

My wife surprised the congregation again with a stunning testimony without repeating the same words she had uttered the previous Sunday. Though she had never sung before in church, she invited the whole assembly to sing along with her the same two songs she kept singing in my ear when I came out of my coma. At the end, she thanked the members of the congregation for their prayers and asked them to keep praying for me, given that I was about to engage in another battle with chemotherapy.

CHAPTER SEVEN

PREPARING FOR THE SECOND BATTLE

During my convalescence, I had to face the prospect that chemotherapy would start soon, given the cancer had already spread. Once I left the hospital, my surgeon urged me to see an oncologist as fast I as could to set up a treatment program. Knowing about the brutal side effects of chemotherapy, some of my family members and friends didn't like the idea. In fact, someone from the church's finance committee drew my attention when she said to me, "Brother Joel, if I were you, I would not go through chemo; that can ruin what the Lord has already done. Rest assured that God has already cured you. Please, don't let the doctors kill you with that poison."

It was not easy for me to make the decision. I was torn between following doctors' orders and heeding fellow Christians' advice. Reluctantly, I called the oncologist's office for an appointment in early December, but her secretary told me she was already booked for the entire month and the earliest appointment available was January 3, 2015. She offered to put me on a waiting list, however, in case a cancellation arose in December. I gladly accepted the January 3rd appointment to buy myself some time, in case I decided to change my mind about getting treatment.

In the meantime, I could hardly ignore regular doctor visits because I kept receiving appointment reminders via telephone. My PCP, for example, insisted on meeting with me December 1st to see how I was doing after my post-operative complications. As he checked my medical report from the hospital, he asked me how soon I would begin chemotherapy. When I let him know that my first visit with my oncologist wouldn't happen until January 3rd, he became deeply concerned. In a last-ditch effort to speed up the treatment process, my PCP made a phone call directly to the oncologist to set up an emergency appointment so I wouldn't have to wait until January 3rd to see her.

Two days later, on December 3rd, my wife and I headed to the Hematology/Oncology

Department to meet with my oncologist to discuss a treatment plan. As a cancer specialist with many years of experience, she sounded quite hopeful that I might completely recover from Stage III cancer. She told me that since the cancer had already metastasized, fluorouracil (5-FU) in combination with oxaliplatin was the best chemotherapy option available. Both medications would be given in the hospital at the same time, over 120 minutes, in separate bags using a Y-line as a 24-hour continuous infusion. An aggressive dose was recommended for 12 cycles every two weeks via a port-a-cath, a tube administering the drugs into a large vein in my chest, in addition to infusions of 5-FU at home through a small pump.

She took time to explain all the risk factors, the side effects and symptoms involved, such as diarrhea, fatigue, weakness, nausea/vomiting, loss of hair, loss of appetite, numbness and tingling in the hands and feet, and discoloration of the skin. My oncologist didn't hesitate to let me know that if severe complications occurred because of the chemotherapy, she would have to stop treatment and Stage III would turn into Stage IV, which is the terminal phase. She was hoping my body would not react badly to the combination regimen, citing an example of an 80-year-old female patient who went through all the cycles without blinking. To me, that was very comforting despite all the bad news I had heard about what chemo could do to people's bodies.

My wife, who was another set of ears in the room, asked the oncologist key questions, such as "What is the likelihood that my husband will be cured after all he has been through already?"

She replied, "Mrs. Doutre, I understand your concern, but the surgeon and I are very optimistic. We agree that your husband has a good chance to recover from cancer."

When my wife inquired about cancer survival statistics for patients who went through the treatment, my oncologist indicated the general statistics for patients who had been cured of Stage III colon cancer after receiving 5-FU and oxaliplatin was 34%. For people with Stage IV, as she mentioned, survival of this adjuvant treatment varied between 20% and 30%.

Having been provided with some not-so-encouraging statistics, I went home to research the efficiency of both drugs and the risks associated with them. First, I found a review article titled "Oxaliplatin with 5-FU or as a Single Agent in Advanced/Metastatic Colorectal

Cancer" published by the Cancer Network Home of the Oncology. This study conducted by Edith P. Mitchell, MD, FACP, on 1,131 patients with metastatic colorectal cancer unveils something positive: for patients with metastatic colorectal cancer and disease progression after treatment with 5-FU and irinotecan chemotherapy, oxaliplatin offers an alternative treatment strategy.

According to Mitchell, the agent is well tolerated and exhibits a manageable toxicity profile. Her observational study also reported an indication of partial remission, though she also identified serious adverse events. One study found that deaths occurred as a result of disease progression, and study-related deaths accounted for less than 1% of mortality. The most frequently observed side effects included nausea, vomiting, diarrhea, dehydration, neutropenia, fevers, seizure, altered mental status, cramping, spasm, and others. (Mitchell, December 2000)

As I went further in my research, I came across some horrific stories posted on a few websites by family members of cancer patients who had received 5-FU-based chemotherapy. According to one post on cancercompass.com, someone's father died from severe diarrhea from 5-FU. Following his first treatment, he started developing diarrhea every hour, then later every 15 minutes. He was rushed to the hospital for dehydration. The nightmare continued for the next four days with the doctors trying unsuccessfully to stop the diarrhea before the patient succumbed the following week.

Another post on cancercompass.com describes the health condition of a middle-aged woman who received her first dose of 5-FU after being diagnosed with breast cancer. Due to the severe reaction she had from the treatment, she was admitted to the hospital 11 days later and diagnosed with Grade IV leucopenia, thrombocytopenia, stomatitis, mucositis, and diarrhea. This breast cancer patient spent 13 days in the hospital and seemingly suffered from memory loss the first seven days. Four weeks later, she was unable to do what she used to do prior to the chemo because of intense fatigue. Eventually, she was informed that she had an enzyme deficiency, which made her body unable to metabolize the 5-FU. After reading this particular post, I started to wonder why my oncologist didn't even bother to find out if I had a medical issue that would keep my body from absorbing the 5-FU.

Upon further research, I found that 5-FU could be deadly for cancer patients with a DPD enzyme deficiency. I learned from Wikipedia, the free encyclopedia, that a DPD deficiency is an autosomal recessive metabolic disorder in which there is an absence or a significantly decreased activity of dehydropyrimidine dehydrogenase, an enzyme involved in the metabolism of uracil and thymine. Patients with this condition may develop life-threatening toxicity following exposure to 5-FU.

I also came across an article called "Lethal Outcome of 5-Fluorouracil infusion in a patient with a total DPD deficiency and a double DPYD and UTG1A1 gene mutation" published by the British Pharmacological Society (BPS). In this article, the BPS reports, to their knowledge, the first published case of lethal 5-FU toxicity related to an IVS14+1G>A homozygote mutation in a DPYD gene associated with the TA7/7 homozygote mutation in the in UTGIAI gene promotor. The victim was a 75-year-old male patient who had begun receiving chemotherapy four weeks after surgery. His treatment consisted of oxaliplatin and 5-FU, which was supposed to be repeated every two weeks. The patient, however, developed odynophagia the second day after the first infusion. The following day, his general status started to deteriorate significantly, his renal function worsened, and he developed leucopenia. Despite intensive medical care, as the BPS describes, the patient died two days later, at day 10 after the initial 5-FU infusion.

Thanks to research, I became aware that nearly 8% of the U.S. population has at least partial DPD deficiency and that it is more common among African-Americans than it is among Caucasians. Unfortunately, it is not standard practice to test for a DPD deficiency, even though people who suffered from it had toxic reactions to 5-FU and died. Being of Haitian descent, I didn't know if I fit into that small portion of the U.S. population who has an enzyme deficiency. As a precaution, I chose to ignore my doctors' push for chemotherapy to start mid-December and asked my oncologist to test me for the DPD deficiency first. She had no other choice than to agree to my decision. "Very wise, Mr. Doutre. Very wise," she said.

A week later, I called the Hematology/Oncology Department for the test result and I was told it wasn't on file. It took me close to 10 minutes on the phone to find out that my blood sample collection was lost in the pile on the way to

California from Massachusetts. Consequently, I had to make another trip to the hospital to get my blood drawn again. I didn't mind waiting another week for the test result, which showed no evidence of an enzyme deficiency. It may have been time consuming to go through the process again, but it was wiser to be cautious. As the saying goes, better safe than sorry.

In fact, delaying my treatment until I was cleared for the DPD deficiency was a good thing for me during the holiday season. It gave me the opportunity to share quality time with my three sisters from Montreal, who vowed to spend their Christmas vacation with me in Boston. They couldn't wait to see their big brother, whom they had not seen since October 12th, the day I became comatose. They arrived with joy on Christmas Eve in the afternoon and later accompanied me to church for the four-hour traditional Christmas celebration, followed by the big supper at midnight in the reception hall. The church took the opportunity to extend a warm welcome to my sisters, who in turn thanked members for their moral and spiritual support toward my family during the difficult moments.

Christmas celebrations have always been special to the Doutre family. My siblings and I still exchange gifts during our family time on December 25th, a tradition we have had since we were children growing up together. As adults, it has become our custom to hold a family gathering every Christmas in Montreal where at least 50 extended family members have a chance to reconnect and bond with one another. But this time, due to special circumstances, my three sisters opted to break with the Montreal tradition to be in Boston instead. While they were showering me with gifts, they let me know the greatest Christmas gift they had ever received was my coming back to life. In reality, I was not supposed to live to see Christmas 2014, but God did the impossible. So, I learned to count my blessings every morning and praise Him with every breath I take.

After Christmas season was over and my sisters went back to Canada, I was getting in the mood for the New Year's Eve celebration. The arrival of 2015 could not find me anywhere other than the local church for an elaborate night of worship. This was a perfect occasion to express my appreciation and give thanks to the Lord with a grateful heart, instead of sitting in front of a TV, watching Dick Clark's New Year's Rocking Eve. Because Haitian Independence Day is celebrated on January 1st, the congregation headed to the church cafeteria after midnight to feast on the traditional squash soup to mark the Independence.

CHAPTER EIGHT

FACING ANOTHER TOUGH BATTLE

With the coming of the New Year, I was ready to face an expected serious battle with chemotherapy. This new event was creeping up on me as the days passed by. On Wednesday, January 7, 2015, at 9:00 a.m., I was scheduled to report to my first treatment. Many of my friends were skeptical. Some family members, showing concern, advised me not to go through the process. But I was determined to go ahead, especially when my wife gave me the nod, saying, "Honey, let's get it over with." I decided to go along with the treatment program with no fear, knowing "the only thing we have to fear is fear itself," as President Franklin Delano Roosevelt asserted in his 1933 inaugural speech.

On my first day, I quickly realized the chemo ward was not like a prison. The nurse assigned to administer the treatment through a port-a-cath inserted in my upper chest gave me a pillow and a warm blanket to make me comfortable. Nevertheless, sitting in a chemo chair for four hours, believe me, was no fun. The total time for the session included one hour of waiting for test results to make sure my white blood cell count was okay and another three hours for infusion.

Seeing those sizable cocktail bags hanging over my head was like seeing poison going inside me. I felt as though a lethal injection was peacefully going through my veins. Jokingly, I asked the nurse how long it should take me to cross the great divide. She said, "Don't worry, Mr. Doutre. This is not a death sentence. You are going to live." I took solace in the fact that my wife was with me in the infusion room. Besides, I had a TV in the room and Wi-Fi for my phone. Having the opportunity to order free lunch was one of the perks offered in the chemo ward. After that first session, since my appetite was still intact, I could relish a three-course meal of my choice before leaving the hospital, with a chemo pump that continued the treatment at home for two days.

I was aware I had to make frequent visits to the hospital, something I could not do alone. After taking a Family Medical Leave of Absence

(FMLA) from her state job for my prolonged hospitalizations back in October, my wife found a way to cope with my repeated visits. This time she could apply for intermittent leave to drive me back and forth and care for me. My wife was aware that should things get complicated, she had to make herself available. We didn't hesitate, therefore, to dub the hospital our second home.

From the very beginning, I was doing what I could to help manage the side effects from my chemotherapy. Besides taking standard anti-nausea medications during my chemo sessions every morning and every evening, I made myself a cup of fresh ginger tea to alleviate nausea and vomiting. To reduce the risk of having diarrhea, I stayed away from high-fiber foods such as lettuce, green vegetables, and wheat bread. Moreover, I chose to eat small amounts of soft, bland, low-fiber foods frequently, such as white rice, noodles, white toast, and clear broth made from chicken and vegetables. I also chose to drink clear soda, such as ginger ale.

As my church's 22nd anniversary was approaching, I'd planned to be part of the weekend celebration every evening from January 23rd to January 25th and I didn't want the side effects from the chemo to stand in my way as music director. Since I had minimal side effects after my first treatment, I was hoping my second treatment on January 21st would go just as smoothly. When I asked the chemo nurse whether I would be able to remain active after the second session, she pointed out the steroid injection designed to keep the side effects at bay after each treatment would only last two days in my system.

During my daily devotional time, I asked God to give me the opportunity to participate actively in my church's anniversary celebration without feeling a pinch. Coincidently, one day before my scheduled second session, a local American evangelist along with my pastor knocked on my door and said, "Brother Joel, we come to your house today to praise God and ask Him to give you enough strength for the upcoming celebration." He showed up with his guitar and held a mini-concert in my living room before the three of us prayed together. The moment we had together in God's presence that morning really paid off. I managed to join my congregation for the three-day celebration after going through treatment and getting my pump disconnected two days later.

A week later, the mucous fistula was releasing blood. Without hesitation, I called my surgeon for an urgent appointment. When I got to his office, he took a close look at the stoma and told me not to worry. The surgeon thought he could simply neutralize the blood with a cotton-tipped applicator, turning the affected area a darkish color. He chose to replace the bag attached to the mucous fistula with a large piece of gauze and sent me home.

For some reason, the blood could not be neutralized. Instead, it gradually intensified, forcing me to change the gauze several times overnight. Early in the morning, without calling, I decided to go back to the surgeon's office, thinking he could find a way to stop the bleeding. He proceeded to rub the fistula with Vaseline and put layers of gauze on it. To prevent blood from coming out, he tightly wrapped my belly with a large elastic bandage with a hook closure and sent me home.

In two days, the fistula grew from the size of a quarter to that of an orange. Having seen me for the third time in a week, the surgeon didn't know what to do with that piece of meat on my abdomen. When I asked him why it kept growing, he told me it had become ulcerated as the days passed. He kept turning the infected fistula around and seemed baffled by the situation. The surgeon invited another colleague from the office to take a look at the problem, but he didn't have an answer, and I told my surgeon I wasn't going to leave his office without one. He said he wished he could cut everything off and put my intestines back together to solve the problem. Unfortunately, he realized he would have to wait until the oncologist finished administering my chemotherapy treatments before he could reactivate my system. In the meantime, he sent me home with more Vaseline, gauze, and extra bandages. He promised me he was going seek advice from his colleagues in Texas so he would know what to do.

Effectively, a few days later, the surgical department called me and let me know the surgeon had decided to remove the ulcerated fistula. The date set for this third operation was February 5th at 12:00 p.m., and I needed to arrive by 10:00 a.m. to register and see the pre-surgical nurse. To be honest, I couldn't wait to have that ulcer removed from my abdomen because I was handling too many things at once, so it would be a relief to get this one thing out of the way. Another good thing was the oncologist had to suspend chemotherapy for a month to allow me to go through the operation and give me time to recuperate.

It was a two-hour surgery and I only had to stay overnight for observation. Though I was in pain, I felt such a relief after the operation; my life became a little less complicated. My surgeon told me to be careful when cleaning the skin around the remaining stoma, however, to prevent ulceration. Before I left the hospital, the discharge nurse instructed me to watch for excessive bleeding or drainage at the surgical site, and to pay special attention to my diet to avoid bowel obstruction.

It only took me a few days before I went back to church to participate in and play music in the Sunday worship service. With the bloody fistula gone, I would have to go to the church bathroom only once to empty my colostomy bag should the service last more than three hours. Taking a break from chemotherapy allowed me to eat snacks in the basement and have a moment of fellowship with the church members after the service. Going back home, it gave me great joy to feast on black rice, conch meat, salad, and cake during my son's 17th birthday celebration since I still had my appetite.

My quick recovery from the third operation enabled me to resume chemotherapy on February 25th. Going into my third cycle, I started becoming tired and sore. Nevertheless, the fact that I was given steroids and anti-nausea medication intravenously right before the chemo cocktail kept the side effects minimal early on. Foods such as scrambled eggs, oatmeal, chicken soup, and noodles went down my stomach easily. But my favorite Haitian meals, notably rice and beans, baked turkey and chicken, as well as fried plantain became my worst enemies. Every time I saw these foods, I wanted to vomit. Yet I was longing for one particular food I had not been able to eat in two years: red beans and bulgur wheat. Hence, I asked my mother-in-law to cook for me this meal with sufficient seasoning. That evening, I savored one plate of that tasty bulgur wheat before I went to bed. It was so good that I stuffed myself with two bowls of it the next day at lunch time. Big mistake!

I had completely forgotten if bulgur wheat was bad for my embattled digestive system. Consequently, two hours later, I started feeling chest pains and my stomach was growling. At first, I thought it was just gas. I went to bed to see if it would go away. Suddenly, the phone rang.

It was an elderly woman, reminding me not to forget that her grandson was coming at 4:00 for math tutoring. I told her I was in great pain, but I promised to call her back as soon as the pain faded away. Instead, it worsened. I was about to crash to the ground in agony. But instead of calling the ambulance, I chose to get in touch with my wife at work, who then called two church members attending Bible study -- a quarter of a mile away from my house -- to take me to the ER.

In the nick of time, the two church ladies picked me up and drove me to the ER. As soon as I checked in, I began vomiting profusely in the waiting room. What came out of my stomach was pure bulgur wheat that had not been digested. That made it easy for the housekeeper to pick up the whole thing with a special machine in no time. The floor looked exactly the way it was before I had arrived − not a trace of barf. The vomiting episode qualified me to see the triage nurse without delay, but the doctors were too busy with other patients to take care of me on the spot. So, I had to wait on a stretcher and agonize for nearly an hour. My wife, who had obtained permission from her boss to leave work, came to be with me. She was canvassing the hallway in fury, trying to reach a doctor to stop my pain.

Finally at 9:00 p.m., a doctor became available. He examined me and put me on morphine to ease my pain, which did not respond well to the treatment. He waited another hour before administering a stronger dose of morphine. Since the morphine could not achieve adequate pain relief, I was taken to Radiology for further evaluation. An X-ray and a CT scan quickly revealed I had a bowel obstruction. The blockage that prevented foods, fluids, and gas from moving through my small intestine in the normal way caused severe pain in my abdomen.

To correct the problem, a nasogastric intubation (known as an NG tube) was deemed medically necessary to gain access to my stomach. The NG tube is a plastic tube that is inserted through the nose, past the throat, and into the stomach, to drain the stomach's contents via the tube into a container. Believe me, it's quite painful. I was screaming, gagging, and vomiting in an emesis basin. Oh, I couldn't take it anymore. At one point, I was saying, "Why me, God? Why do I have to go through this again? Let me die."

My wife was crying her eyes out. She said, "Do not despair, honey. Everything will be all right someday."

The doctor together with the nurse had to stop the process halfway to allow me to regain my composure. They told me they were going to try again as soon as they could find me a room in the hospital. I had to spend the whole night in the ER before a room became available at 4:00 a.m. on the seventh floor. The same doctor tried the NG tube again and this time I had no other choice but to go through the whole process. Once the tube reached my stomach, I saw greenish liquids cruising through the catheter into a collection bag. It didn't take me five minutes to breathe a sigh of relief. No more pain!

I had the NG tube hooked to my chest the whole day to evacuate all the debris stuffed in my stomach. I had learned, for sure, a valuable lesson: Never put foods such as bulgur wheat in my mouth. Never again! I could understand why in the afternoon, my surgeon stopped by my room to ask me, "Have you changed your diet lately, Mr. Doutre?" I think he meant to ask me if I had cheated on my diet. Given my situation, however, I could not afford to stray from my diet anymore. On the day of my release from the hospital, the charge nurse made sure she told me what I could eat and what I needed to avoid as a colostomy patient.

As the days went by, I reached treatment #4. The symptoms and side effects from the chemotherapy were getting rough. The chemo darkened my skin and sometimes even turned my face navy blue; sometimes people could hardly recognize me. The skin on my hands peeled. My fingernails and toenails looked as if they were burnt. My hair thinned significantly until it was gone. I lost nearly 40 pounds and looked like someone living with AIDS. My appetite and energy level went down drastically.

Even though my nausea eventually became manageable, I tried to stay away from food because every time something entered my mouth, I would start vomiting. I threw up every time I brushed my teeth. I became so weak I could hardly empty my colostomy bag at night. There were instances when I fell in the bathroom, attempting to change or unload my pouch. I had to clean up the mess myself because I didn't want to disturb my wife as she was asleep. Diarrhea was controllable with Imodium, but my general weakness required me to be hospitalized every two weeks.

I also had to deal with the cold temperature during the winter season. Even for healthy people, coping with the chilly days of winter 2014 was unbearable. Ever since January when my treatment began, my oncologist warned me about extreme cold sensitivity. Whenever I went outside, I needed to wear gloves and a hat and cover my whole face with a scarf, in addition to wearing a heavy coat, solid socks, and shoes. Cold sensitivity also forced me to drink fluids at room temperature, especially the first five days after each infusion. Otherwise, my body would have become completely numb.

I was also cautioned to stay away from people who had colds or other infections and avoid crowds as much as possible. But that did not stop me from going to church every Sunday, unless I was kept in the hospital. As God's servant and the head of the music department, I would not have felt comfortable staying away on the Lord's Day. In good days and bad days, my passion to worship, play guitar, and lead would not waver. But with all the burdens I had to carry and the little physical strength I had left, I could only play sitting down. My son on the drums, the other young musicians on the bass guitar, and the two keyboard players managed to follow my lead, knowing that poor performance was not in my playbook. I wanted to convey a strong message to my youths -- Christians involved in God's ministry should take their jobs seriously in sickness and in health.

Frankly, I don't really know how to explain how I was able to make it to church every Sunday because I could barely walk and the chemotherapy was taking a big toll on my strength. There were instances when my wife had to hold me on one side and my son on the other to get me inside the church. In order to play the guitar, someone had to pull it out of the case and hand it to me. Once I started playing, I began regaining my strength because worshiping through songs builds up others, as Paul says in Ephesians 5:19: "Speaking to one another with psalms, hymns, and songs from the Spirit. Sing and make music from your heart to the Lord." Participating actively in the worship service felt like good therapy to me; it helped me keep the faith, believing my perseverance would pay off. "God is not unjust," says Paul, "He will not forget your work and the love you have shown Him as you have helped His people and continue to help them." (Hebrews 6:10)

Going back home, I had to face the grim reality that I was getting weaker and weaker. I reached a point where the treatment was killing me faster than the cancer. I had lost half of my body mass and I had no food inside me because I couldn't eat anymore. I had no other choice, therefore, than to stay in bed all day, except on Sundays when I felt the urge to attend worship service.

Back from church on a Sunday afternoon, I desperately asked my wife to fix one of my favorite dishes for me -- white rice, bean sauce, and baked turkey with gravy. On a normal day, I would dig into that precious meal and finish the whole thing in less than ten minutes. But, after taking my first spoon, it was like ingesting a foul-tasting medicine. Quickly, my wife handed me a bedpan to gag on whatever I had left inside. She had to rush me to the ER and a three-day hospitalization was required to keep me alive for the next treatment cycle the following week.

When I showed up at the hospital on May 6th for another cycle, I looked so bad that the chemo nurse offered me the opportunity to skip the treatment and wait another week. But to my peril I decided to get treatment #8 with four more to go. Since the blood test result indicated my white blood count was somewhat low, my oncologist deemed it necessary to send me to the walk-in clinic for a booster shot. When I went back to the chemo ward later on, I let the nurse know I was bold enough to withstand the brunt of the treatment. I was about to pay a big price for my bravado.

Over the next few days, diarrhea coupled with abdominal pain came back in full force. On a temporary basis, I succeeded in stopping the diarrhea with Imodium. That gave me enough latitude to go to the Sunday worship service, even though the abdominal pain persisted. When my wife asked me if I had enough strength to go to church, I told her the truth about the continuing pain lingering all over my body. "Don't you think, honey, I should take you to the emergency room right now?" she asked me. I told her I would prefer that she take me the day after instead because I didn't want to miss the Sunday service.

First thing Monday morning, I called the Hematology/Oncology Department to complain about my abdominal pain and general weakness. The doctor on call didn't hesitate to ask me to come in right away. My wife, who always made herself available (day and night), rushed me to the ER. Upon arrival, I was hooked to IV fluids because I was completely dehydrated. According to the ER doctor, if I had waited much longer, it would have been too late. Immediately, I was admitted because I already looked like a zombie.

Meanwhile, a foul-smelling diarrhea (that smelled like rotten eggs) occurred with rapid frequency, forcing nurses to empty my colostomy bag repeatedly. At night, my wife had to stay awake to vacate the watery stool from my pouch at least every hour because the night-shift staff would hardly come around or not at all to do the task. She kept asking doctors why the diarrhea stank so bad; a stool sample sent to the lab later revealed I had Clostridium difficile (or C. diff) as a result of Colitis, forcing medical staff and visitors to wear special gowns and masks before entering my room.

On the third day, my oncologist stopped by my room to watch me die slowly. First, she apologized for the strong dose of 5-FU that ended up damaging my intestine, according to additional tests performed in Radiology. She also came to notify me of her formal decision to stop the treatment. "Mr. Doutre, I'd rather keep you alive for a while instead of killing you right now," she said.

"What about radiation?" asked my wife.

The oncologist replied, "There is nothing radiation can do for your husband's type of cancer."

Well, what did that mean to friends and family members? Surely, a death sentence. My sisters, who didn't want to lose another brother, had tears in their eyes when they saw me lying between life and death a second time.

I never lost faith in my Lord because He never starts something He cannot finish. God is called the author and the finisher of our faith. Sometimes, the enemy would remind me of others who had died of Stage III colon cancer and wanted me to believe the cancer would eat me away. Despite the miracle Jesus performed on me in October when I was in a coma, my adversary used my new medical report to cast doubt and discouragement into my heart. I strongly believed God was going to complete my incompletions and I would not go to my grave without seeing my dreams come to pass, even the secret petitions of my heart.

Lying in a hospital bed and receiving chemotherapy treatments could not achieve anything other than wreaking havoc in my body, but it gave me the opportunity to put my money where my mouth is. I always preach what I believe. One of my last sermons at church was about faith, without which it is impossible to please God, according to Hebrews 11:6. Why should I preach about faith if I can't put my faith in action in the face of adversity? If I believe God exists and rewards those who put their faith in Him, there is no reason I should doubt what God can do. Many of us feel that God is silent at times. Sometimes when we want to hear from God it seems that all heaven is silent. Nevertheless, I firmly believed that God was aware of what was happening to me and that there is no inability with Him.

Faith was what kept me going during my 12-day stay in the hospital, where doctors desperately tried to stop one of my episodes of diarrhea lasting 11 consecutive days while I was on IV fluids. Faith was what gave me confidence in God when no treatment could be found to cure my cancer. Faith was what provided me the assurance that nothing is impossible for those who believe in God. Faith was what got me through the painful days until doctors cleared me to leave the hospital.

CHAPTER NINE

LEVELS OF FUNCTIONAL ABILITY REGARDLESS OF THE ODDS

I resumed my normal church activities such as Bible studies, prayer meetings, and Sunday services as I continued to battle the disease, but this time with minimal symptoms and side effects. The peripheral neuropathy involving numbing and tingling in both feet and hands did not impair my regular function. Compared to all the trauma my body had to endure for a long time, the peripheral neuropathy was only a small nuisance. These are small troubles for a Christian as the Apostle Paul declares in 2 Corinthians 4:15: "For our light and temporary affliction is producing for us an eternal glory that far outweighs our troubles."

As I continued to get stronger after the cessation of chemotherapy, I could easily drive 20 miles back and forth to the radio station and resume what I do best: broadcasting, public service ads (PSAs), music promotion, and interviews. In fact, the passion I found in broadcasting was rousing energy in me day after day. Spending time with a few colleagues sharing the same passion for God's service at the station was really therapeutic. I went to the radio station at least twice a week.

As my taste buds were being restored to their full potential, I didn't turn down invitations to barbecue events from friends. I thought putting some animal protein in my body was a great way to regain the necessary weight I needed to get back in shape. In the early summer months, I would attend a different cookout every weekend for graduations or birthday celebrations. To be honest, I could not resist the grill after chemotherapy had stopped. The closer to the grill I stayed, the bigger my appetite grew. I recall some instances when I ingested two burgers, two hotdogs, and three drumsticks all in one cookout, and some of my friends said, "Wow! He can eat."

Well, I thought, *a good appetite is a sign of good health.* I had to wait and see, however, how all that eating would affect my body. Turns out, I went from 130 to 160 pounds by July 1st.

I made the decision to skip a 4th of July cookout because my wife asked me not to eat so much meat. But how did she know I was shoving too much meat down my throat if she was never with me at those barbecues? Well, it only took one traitor, none other than the grill operator from church, to tell my wife I had been ingesting too many drumsticks, burgers, and hotdogs at barbecues. She decided to call the authorities (my siblings from Montreal) to tell on me, as if they were my bosses. What a snitch! My sisters, who kept checking on me every day to make sure I was doing the right things, told me to ease up on burgers and hotdogs and stick with salads, green vegetables, and whole grains if I wanted to live longer. Advice well taken.

Anyway, the drumsticks, burgers, and hotdogs I had overindulged myself with in the early summer months provided me enough protein to get bigger and stronger. I decided to make a triumphant comeback, therefore, to hosting radio programs and emceeing events. As the 32nd anniversary of my radio ministry was approaching, a lot of preparation was underway to make the celebration a success with a colorful play, along with dance and music performances by the most talented artists in the Christian community. I thought I was ready for the big celebration and I could not wait to face the public.

Eventually, on Sunday, August 9th, nearly a thousand people gathered at John Hancock Hall in Boston to celebrate the 32 years of *Echo Evangélique*. During the first hour of the show, emceed by my mentor, Jean Joseph Normil, I was still back stage with the actors enjoying the musical performance of Maggie Blanchard, one of the most reputed female artists living in Montreal.

Around 7:15, the big moment came. It was my turn to make my appearance on stage. When Normil introduced me as another Lazarus who had come back from the dead, the whole audience went crazy. Everybody was clapping and cheering; many people from the audience were uttering words of praise like "Alleluia" and "God is good all the time." As I received a standing ovation, I had to let the public express their joy of seeing me back before I could start speaking.

I started by alluding to the severity of Epaphroditus' illness, which Paul mentioned in Philippians 2:27, to tell the audience I was sick and near death, and that thanks to their prayers, God had mercy on me. When I saw the way people responded, it seemed they were ready to listen to my story for a good amount of time. But since a two-hour play was scheduled for the evening, in less than 10 minutes, I managed to give an account of my bad experiences with the doctors and tell the audience how God intervened to save me.

At the end of the evening, one of the female fans approached me and said, "Brother Joel, you brought the whole house down with your vibrant testimony." Another lady admitted that my 10-minute testimony alone was worth the $40 she had paid for the event. According to many people from the audience, my testimony was nothing short of God's faithfulness and happened to be the climax of the 32nd anniversary celebration.

The day after the celebration, I went for a visit with my oncologist. I received high marks for taking good care of myself. She told me I didn't look like the same person she had seen back in May at the hospital when I was dying from the debilitating side effects of chemotherapy. "You really scared me, Mr. Doutre," she said. "I thought you had no chance of survival. Now, look at you!"

When the nurse practitioner invited me to step on the weight scale, I was up to 170 – a 40-pound gain from May. As she gave me the thumbs up for being able to recover that fast from a weight deficit, she indicated it was time for me to set up an appointment with my surgeon to talk about the reversal operation. She gladly escorted me to the front desk and asked her secretary to call my surgeon's office to schedule an appointment on my behalf as soon as mid-August.

My surgeon, who had not seen me in five months, had the same reaction to my improved state as the oncologist. He could not believe how different I looked compared to the last time he had seen me when he had to operate on me a third time because of my ulcerated fistula.

Following a 15-minute visit, he sent me home and told me to expect a phone call from his surgical coordinator to give me an exact date for the last surgery, designed to reactivate my intestinal system. Being a colostomy bag carrier for more than ten months, the reversal operation could not come soon enough so I could have my normal life back.

I found myself getting impatient when I received no call a few days later regarding the scheduling of my final operation. When I phoned the surgeon's office to find out if there was a change of plans, I was told the surgical coordinator in charge of the scheduling was off for a week. So, I had to wait for her to come back from vacation.

Meanwhile, my sisters in Canada were planning to have their traditional family barbecue in the same month of August. When they called to inform me of their decision to hold it on Saturday, August 22nd, I wasn't sure I would be there for the event. But as soon as I found out my last surgery was scheduled on Thursday, August 27th, I called my sisters to let them know I was coming and I wanted this to be a surprise to the rest of the family. I knew they were very good at keeping secrets and they would not tell a soul about my trip to Montreal for the traditional barbecue.

For the first time, I was traveling long distance with a colostomy bag. But being a carrier for a long period of time enabled me to make some life adjustments. It became routine that after three hours tops I had to find a bathroom to empty the pouch. My wife, who was the designated driver, occasionally asked me, "Honey, have you checked your bag?" From experience, and with a little sniff, she could tell when there was a leak or when the bag had reached full capacity.

Having reached Vermont on I-89 North, she proceeded to Exit 8 toward Montpelier, the capital city, to take a bathroom break at a gas station to avoid a bag blowout. Otherwise, it would be a real embarrassment for the whole family in presence of the pastor's wife, who was also riding with us. But since I hadn't eaten much the day before, this was the only bathroom break I needed before we reached our destination. When I got to my sisters' house in Saint Hubert, I was still clean as a whistle.

On Saturday, the relatives who lived the closest to the barbeque site arrived. They were the first to see my wife that day and tried to comfort her, saying, "Poor thing, you came anyway without Joel. We're very sorry he couldn't make it this year." They had no idea I was hiding in the basement.

Minutes later, they received the biggest surprise of their lives when I made my spectacular entrance on the barbecue stage, looking like a million bucks. One of my sisters-in- law said, "Joel, you almost gave me a heart attack. I never thought for a minute you could be here, knowing how sick you are." I told her I wouldn't have missed the family barbecue for the world. As everybody was paying attention to me, my wife, who never left her camera behind, turned my grand entrance into a Kodak moment. It was one of the greatest moments I have ever spent with the entire family and I didn't regret this trip to Canada before my last surgery at all.

The time to get rid of my colostomy bag was approaching and I couldn't wait to get back to the hospital. Unlike people who are anxious at the thought of having surgery, I was looking forward to having my colostomy reversed. Even though I was strong enough to cope with the troubles of daily life for an extended period of time, I wanted to be free of my stoma emptying waste whenever it pleased.

Going through the emotional stress for almost a year would have been devastating, had it not been for God's assistance. Thanks to the presence of the Holy Spirit in my life, I didn't appear withdrawn from anyone and I was still able to go to church and do my radio activities. One of my colleagues would often ask me, "Joel, how do you deal with this? I would go crazy if I was the one in this situation."

I always replied, "No matter the situation, I relied on God's promise." I just had to wait for the appointed time to have a new beginning.

CHAPTER TEN

ENTERING THE FINAL PHASE OF THE JOURNEY

On Thursday, August 27th, my season of trials was about to end, but it didn't want to leave without a fight. In my mind, my reversal operation was a relatively minor procedure and it was supposed to go smoothly. I was so calm that I fell asleep even before I went to the operating room at 2:00 p.m. But when I woke up at 6:30 in the recovery room, I felt as if I had just been hit by a truck. I had so much pain that I instantly begged for a strong painkiller. In a matter of minutes, the medical staff was able to keep my postsurgical pain under control.

As I moved to my regular room, I was given the power to control my pain through a computerized pump called the patient-controlled analgesia pump (PCP), connected directly to my intravenous (IV) line. After every ten minutes, I could self-administer an additional dose of hydromorphone by pressing a button.

As the pain subsided, another unwelcome situation surfaced on my abdomen. Within two days following the surgery, my stomach had grown to the size of that of a pregnant woman. The abdominal distention, according to the surgical team, occurred because the large intestine had fallen asleep after the resection and had become too lazy after a long period of time. One of the surgeons confided in me that the reconnection of the bowels had not been an easy task for her to carry out. From what she said, she went to great lengths to remove multiple scars from the large intestine before she could reconnect the two bowels. The real question was, how were they going to get rid of so much bloating and intestinal gas? I was told to wait and the distention would run its course in a matter of days.

On Sunday, August 30th, false hope arrived when I felt the urge to pass gas and have a bowel movement at the same time. I thought the ability to pass gas and stool was a clear sign of my intestines waking up for good. As I headed to the bathroom, the doctor in charge was put on notice. She told the nurse she didn't think the time was appropriate and it would take me more than three days before passing stool. In fact, she was right. When the nurse came to inspect, all she found in the toilet was pure blood. Anyway, it was comforting to know that passing blood after this type of surgery was normal and should not be a concern.

Meanwhile, I could not tolerate the accumulation of fluids in my abdominal cavity. Instead of becoming less bloated, my belly was ready to blow up, and food became my worst enemy. Waiting for the swelling in my stomach to lessen was no longer an option when I realized I was developing a high fever, which could have indicated infection. I asked one of the female doctors if there was something she could do to solve the problem because I didn't want to take the chance of waiting for the distention to run its course. I was so desperate that I felt obligated to tell the female doctor the following anecdote:

"Once upon time, there was a poor elderly man in Haiti's countryside, who had gone a few days without eating because of food shortages. Thanks to a group of American missionaries, who brought food to the region, the octogenarian found more than enough to eat. But he ate so much that his belly was about to explode.

Fortunately, someone brought the best cleanser in the Haitian culture, an enema bag called *bòk*, containing natural medicine fluids. They laid him straight on the floor and inserted the enema tube into his rectum. It didn't take the old man long to evacuate into the missionaries' faces."

"Interesting story," said the doctor. After she laughed for a while, she added, "In the medical culture, we have something classier, called the NG tube, but it's painful."

Since I had already been through the procedure because of an intestinal obstruction back in March, I told her I was ready to go through it again. Immediately, she went to the next room to grab the necessary equipment and came back with two nurses to assist her with the procedure. True, I was in agonizing pain, gagging and screaming my head off. But once the tube reached down the esophagus and into the stomach, I breathed a sigh of relief, having seen a bunch of green liquids cruising through the tube, landing in the container. I dubbed this a real phenomenon because it allowed the bloating to go down significantly in a short period of time. The tube had to be left attached for continuous drainage, however. During that evening and well into the night, a total of three liters of fluids were ejected into the collection bag.

It took the NG tube the next three days to absorb and completely suck out the excessive accumulation of fluids from my stomach. At times, it was a real discomfort dealing with the tube hurting my nose and throat, but the result was so much better than the pain, food deprivation, and sleepless nights I had to go through. I wondered how long it would take for my distention to run its course if I didn't voluntarily accept the NG tube treatment. I strongly believed it was a good call on my part, enabling me to avoid a repeat of the unfortunate October 12, 2014, episode, leading to a medically induced coma. This time, I was kept in the hospital for only 12 days.

For the first time in 11 months, I was able to live a normal life. Getting back the ability to move my bowel the regular way was a blessing I have learned to appreciate. I had taken it for granted until I was deprived of it. I genuinely sympathize with those who have to spend the rest of their lives with a colostomy bag. Unfortunately, for people who have the whole rectum removed, it is a permanent operation. But there is a great blessing for anyone who has to wear the bag continuously: they get to live, and life is precious.

Since the oncologist chose to stop treatment because of the aggressive and toxic nature of the drugs that had nearly ended my life back in May, I continued to rely on God's intervention for a complete cure. In fact, relying on God was my only alternative after my doctors failed to eradicate my metastatic lesions through chemotherapy, even though the original cancer had been surgically removed. Paul makes sense in Philippians 1:6 when he says, "For I am confident of this, that he who began the good work in you will carry it to completion until the day of Christ Jesus." My God is not in the habit of starting something and not finishing it. I had no doubt that if God led me through the dark journeys, He definitely had a plan to keep me alive long enough to accomplish a mission on earth I had not finished yet. Everything I went through that year helped me build and increase my reliance on God in good as well as bad days.

After suffering for a year with a cancer whose treatment was really cruel with all the symptoms and complications, nothing scared me anymore. Abdominal pain, lung failure, kidney failure, and sepsis caused by doctors' gross negligence during the initial surgery back on October 8, 2014, followed by chemotherapy side effects such as diarrhea, vomiting, weight loss, and general weakness requiring by-weekly hospitalization, were part of the permissive will of God. My wife, who was in the most desperate situation back then, with tears in her eyes, has come to believe that God's ear was not too dull to save and deliver me, as people kept praying for my full recovery. In fact, she was the one who convinced me to ask my oncologist to run a CT scan that would confirm what God has already done.

Through my nurse practitioner, during a follow-up visit, I petitioned my oncologist for a CT scan. Since my last scan that still showed cancerous lesions in certain organs was performed back in May 2015, I had to wait another six months for my health insurance to authorize coverage for another such exam. Effectively, a repeat of the examination of the abdomen and pelvis was scheduled on Monday, November 30, 2015, at 12:30 p.m.

In spite of her work schedule, my wife wanted to be there. In fact, she never missed a single medical appointment with me, and asked all sorts of questions. On that day, she pressured me to be at Central Registration early in order to make it to the Radiology Department on time. There was no reason to rush, however, because other patients who had emergency exams had to go ahead of me. I managed to get on that machine at 2:00 p.m. and by 3:00 I was already home, waiting to go back to the oncologist for the result on December 2nd.

It looked as if the doctor couldn't wait to give me the verdict. On the same afternoon I had the examination, I received a phone call from my oncologist at 5:30, telling me she couldn't wait until Wednesday to give me the news and she couldn't believe what she saw on the CT scan. "To tell you the truth, Mr. Doutre, I was not expecting this result," she explained. According to her, the CT scan showed no signs of cancer. She even commented, "I don't know what you've been doing. But whatever you've been doing really works. Now, you are cancer free. Congratulations!"

When I got off the phone, all I wanted to do was take my clothes off, run along the street, and shout "Hallelujah and Praise the Lord!" Unfortunately, it was too cold that evening. Since my wife was not home, the best thing I could do was drive to a home prayer meeting a few blocks from my house. There, I was able to share the good news with a group of people, including my pastor, and some fervent church members.

It wasn't until 9:00 when I went back home that I surprised my wife with the stunning result. Believe me, it was more than a celebration for both of us because the fight with cancer was finally over. On that memorable day, Monday, November 30, 2015, when my oncologist gave me a clean bill of health, I officially reached the end of my extended journey.

CONCLUSION

WHAT IT TAKES TO BE A FULL-GROWN CHRISTIAN

At the end of my long journey, it is imperative to reiterate that the God of Abraham, Isaac, and Jacob is the God of all generations. During that difficult journey, I learned to lean on Him and trust Him when the battle seemed more than I could handle. What I went through could be likened to the bitter waters of Marah in the Book of Exodus, recounting the plight of the Israelites who had been wandering in the desert for three days without water. But the Lord has genuinely proved to me that He is still Jehovah-Jireh (the Lord who provides) and Jehovah-Rapha (the Lord who heals). Locked in a coma after an operation went wrong, I had little hope of surviving. And a miracle did eventually occur. The Lord lifted me out of death. The water that tasted bitter did become sweet.

Receiving total healing from the Lord can take a long time. Of course, for some of us, God provides a quick fix. But for others such as the blind man in Mark 8:22-25, who could "see men like trees, walking" after Jesus touched him the first time, complete healing is not instantaneous. If Jesus put His hands on the blind man's eyes a second time to make him see everyone clearly, my dear Lord deemed it necessary to make another intervention later on in my favor to make me whole and healthy when chemotherapy could not eradicate my cancer.

As a member of the Body of Christ, I also realized that God wanted me to go through pain and suffering over that year. He truly helped me see those afflictions as opportunities to mature, knowing that suffering produces perseverance. As the Apostle James argues in James 1:4, "Let perseverance finish its work so that you may be mature and complete, not lacking anything." I understand that God uses tough times to mold and shape Christian lives, like clay in the potter's hands.

Throughout my afflictions, the Lord taught me to appreciate the value of good health, which is our most precious possession. It is a gift from God to man. Don't get me wrong when I quote the

Apostle Paul in 1 Corinthians 15:19: "If only for this life we have hope in Christ, we are of all people most to be pitied." To live for eternity, God provides spiritual healing through His Son, which is available to all people. Voluntarily, Jesus endured the worst pain and suffered a shameful death to provide the greatest remedy to mankind as foretold by Isaiah the Prophet, more than 700 years before the Savior was born:

He was despised and rejected by mankind, a man of suffering, and familiar with pain. Like one from whom people hide their faces, he was despised, and we held him in low esteem. Surely he took up our pain and bore our suffering, yet we considered him punished by God, stricken by him, and afflicted. But he was pierced for our transgressions, he was crushed for our iniquities: the punishment that brought us peace was on him, and by his wounds we are healed. (Isaiah 53:3-5)

Having been justified through faith, I continue to rejoice in the Lord. I don't rejoice because I am healed physically. I rejoice because I have been blessed with the greatest gift: eternal salvation, which is only for those who believe in Jesus as a result of His finished work on the cross of Calvary. Because of Calvary, as believers we have been brought into a wonderful relationship with the great Jehovah, having escaped God's anger and condemnation. Hence, we are no longer God's bitter enemy, but God's friend and beloved child, living an abundant life.

But the fact that our life is full of purpose, potential, and joy, doesn't mean that Christian living is easy. Since the life of Christ on earth had its pitfalls, Christian living is not all sunshine and roses. We have to deal with obstacles day in and day out. As Jesus' disciples, "we are troubled on every side, yet not distressed" notes the Apostle Paul, "perplexed, but not in despair; persecuted, but not forsaken; cast down, but not destroyed." With that being said, our life is compared to that of a soldier on active service. Once we become Christians, we ought to be ready for war. It's not a matter of "if" trials happen but "when" trials happen.

Never before had I lived with illnesses requiring hospitalizations and surgeries. I was always boasting about being one of the healthiest members of my family. I had never hesitated to tell my fellow Christians that God never let me go under the knife, when I knew of other people who had been operated on too many times. Nevertheless, when I took the time to read the words of the prophets and the apostles, who were great sufferers, I knew, sooner or later, my life would take a major hit. I became mindful that in order to acquire the status of a full-grown Christian, I needed to go through afflictions. "Many are the afflictions of the righteous," says David in Psalm 34:19, "but the Lord delivers him from all."

SELECT BIBLIOGRAPHY

- British Pharmacological Society (2011). Lethal Outcome of 5-Fluorouracil infusion in a patient with a total DPD deficiency and a double DPYD and UTG1A1 gene mutation. Retrieved December 5th, 2014 from onlinelibrary.wiley.com

- Cancer Compass Message Board (2014). Posts Retrieved December, 3rd 2014 from cancercompass.com

- Desmond, R et al. (2006). Increase Prevalence of Dehydropyrimidine Dehydrogenase Deficiency in African-Americans with Caucasians. Article in Clinical Cancer Research 12(18):5491-5. Source: PubMed.

- Jean Baptiste, F (2016). Mémoire Parlante des Leaders Evangéliques Haïtiens. Regards bienveillants par Jonel Dalexis (Vol. 1, p. 194). Publication: JEBCA Editions.

- Machover D, Diaz-Rubio E, et al (1996). Two consecutive phase II studies of oxiplatin (L-OHP) for treatment of patients with advanced colorectal carcinoma who were resistant to previous treatment with fluoropyrimidines. Ann Oncol 7:95-98.

- Mitchell, Edith P. (December, 2000). Oxaliplatin with 5-FU or as a Single Agent in Advanced/Metastatic Colorectal Cancer. , Cancer Network Home of the Oncology.

- Saltz LB, Locker PK, Pirotta N, et al (1999). Weekly irinotecan (CPT – 11), leuvorin (LV), and fluorouracil (FU) is superior to daily x 5 LV/FU in patients (PTS) with previously untreated metastatic colorectal cancer (CRC) (abstract 898). Proc Am Soc Clin Biol 18:233a.
- Wikipedia, the Free Encyclopedia (2011). DPD Deficiency: Putting it all in one place. Retrieved December 4th, 2014 from dpd-deficiency.com/facts/facts.html